THE NAKED TRUTH

THE NAKED TRUTH

A MEMOIR

DANIELLE STAUB

WITH STEVEN PRIGGÉ

GALLERY BOOKS

NEW YORK   LONDON   TORONTO   SYDNEY

Note to Readers:
This work is a memoir. Events, actions, experiences, and their consequences over a period of years have been retold as the author presently recollects them. Some names and identifying characteristics have been changed, and some dialogue has been re-created from memory. Some scenes are composites of events, and the time-line for some events has been compressed.

G

Gallery Books
A Division of Simon & Schuster, Inc.
1230 Avenue of the Americas
New York, NY 10020

Copyright © 2010 by Danielle Staub

First Gallery Books hardcover edition May 2010

GALLERY BOOKS and colophon are trademarks of Simon & Schuster, Inc.

For information about special discounts for bulk purchases, please contact Simon & Schuster Special Sales at 1-866-506-1949 or business@simonandschuster.com.

The Simon & Schuster Speakers Bureau can bring authors to your live event. For more information or to book an event, contact the Simon & Schuster Speakers Bureau at 1-866-248-3049 or visit our website at www.simonspeakers.com.

Designed by Jaime Putorti

Manufactured in the United States of America

10   9   8   7   6   5   4   3   2   1

Library of Congress Cataloging-in-Publication Data is available.

ISBN 978-1-4391-8289-5
ISBN 978-1-4391-8291-8 (ebook)

For my daughters, Christine and Jillian,
who hold the key to my heart

*If I can stop one Heart from
breaking, I shall not live in vain.*

—EMILY DICKINSON

CONTENTS

CONTENTS

INTRODUCTION

The headline on the flyer handed to me at the Chateau hair salon in Franklin Lakes, New Jersey, said "Jersey Girls: My Fabulous Life." It was advertising the casting of a new televised reality show, and the flyer created quite a buzz among all the local girls, who imagined that their "fabulous" suburban lives would fascinate audiences everywhere. My reaction was quite the opposite: "My life sucks, so no thanks."

Six months later, I was again approached about appearing on the reality show. The only show airing on Bravo within the *Housewives* franchise at the time was *The Real Housewives of Orange County* and I hadn't seen it, but it had gotten a stamp of approval from my eldest daughter, Christine (who has become my "go-to" girlfriend for all of my big decisions), so I checked the show out for myself. I definitely liked what I saw.

After viewing an episode, I found it offered refreshing insight into families as well as friendships among married and single women alike. Single moms on the show were going through their problems while getting advice and support from their castmates. This made me think I should consider participating in the show.

In the beginning, I believed being on *The Real Housewives of New Jersey* was going to be an uplifting, quirky, fun, joining-of-the-hands experience that would perhaps entail a little drama shared by all of us. I soon found out how wrong I was. I became the focus of a character attack delivered at the hands of those who would, I thought, be holding mine in friendship. As the first season played out, my castmates' biggest source of ammunition was a book (that came to be referred to as "*the book*")—the exposé written about my first husband, Kevin Maher.

Ironically, being exposed on TV forced me to reconcile my present with my past and realize that those experiences, for better or worse, made me who I am today. As I dealt with the scrutiny of my castmates, something clicked. People were taking so much interest in someone else's take on my life that I decided they would perhaps like to know how it had *really* happened. And my fellow housewives had no right to turn what was my tortured past into the present. I realized that if the public had this much interest in my life, then it was time that I told my story in my own words. There are no two sides to one's life story. If you didn't live it, it's not yours to speak of.

don't want to pretend or claim to be a voice for every house-wife. But I have a voice and I intend to use it. I will lend my life as an example for others.

I get notes every day from people who pour their hearts out to me about their own challenges and how they can re-late to my life's struggles on many levels. These are the people whom I wrote this book for, as well as my children and myself. Every story that's been written about me—and there have been a lot—has been edited. This book is the *unedited* version of my life. What you read in the following chapters is what happened the way I remember it.

In this memoir, I'm finally baring it all. The title, *The Naked Truth*, doesn't refer to being naked without clothing. It means naked as in stripped down and laid bare. It means naked with-out skin—totally raw to the bone. That's exactly what this book is. No matter what has happened in my life, good or bad, I am now in a place where I can make some sense out of it and hopefully help some others to do the same. It's time to set the record straight and correct all the lies. If hell hath no fury like a woman scorned, then hell is a quaint suburb in New Jersey and the woman scorned is resident housewife Danielle Staub.

You either love me or you hate me, there is no in-between. But people *are* going to pay attention when I'm around.

THE NAKED TRUTH

1

LIFE BEFORE BIRTH

didn't need my mother and father to tell me I was adopted. I figured it out for myself. When I was five years old, I sat down on the couch in the living room and said matter-of-factly to my mother, "I don't look like you. I don't act like you. I don't talk like you. I don't look like anyone in our family. Who am I?"

I was born in the summer of 1962, in the United States. It was the era of JFK, the year of the Rolling Stones' first performance, and the year Marilyn Monroe suffered an untimely death. It was also the year my mother traveled all the way from Italy to America to give birth to me.

Everything I understand to be true about my birth family is just stories I've heard. I haven't been able to confirm anything—

not even by birth mother's name. As the story was told to me, my birth mother grew up in an extremely strict Sicilian household. She was born into a big family of devout Catholics. In those days, especially in Italy, the rules of the Catholic Church were extremely strict and unquestioningly followed, almost like laws. Out-of-wedlock pregnancies were highly unacceptable. If a woman had a child out of wedlock, she and her entire family would be looked down upon and ostracized from the community; they would even be excommunicated from the Church.

So, when my mother got pregnant as an unmarried teen, it created much chaos and dissension within her immediate family. The Russos (my biological mother's maiden name was Russo, from what I was told) were a family of much power and wealth and social status in Sicily—so much so that I have been told that the family was "connected" in the true sense of the word.

My mother was fourteen years old when she met my birth father, who was then nineteen. They had consensual and unprotected sex. The result: me. This love affair between them caused an uproar within my mother's family. Once my mother's situation came to light, my grandparents concluded that my mother would have to leave Italy as soon as her pregnancy started showing. My aunt would escort her to the United States to give birth to me. If the pregnancy wasn't handled privately and secretly, it would be a disgrace to the entire Russo family. As a mother of two daughters, I wonder what my grandmother's position was in all of this. Why didn't she stop my grandfather from sending my mother to America and making her give me away? Did she even have a say, or was she helpless because she was living in a society dominated by men? How did my mother's family explain to everyone in Italy why my mother and my aunt were going away to America for all those months? Is all of this true? I have so many questions about this aspect of my family—my existence—that may never be answered.

I was told that my father was actually killed for getting my mother pregnant. *Killed?* If it's true, I'd have to think that my father's murder was a reflection of the ignorance and tendency toward violence that was prevalent in that part of Italy at that time, and the hypocrisy of his death is quite clear to me: you gain one life but lose another for no valid reason.

In a scene in *The Godfather*, Michael Corleone (played by Al Pacino) kills a crooked police sergeant in New York and goes to Italy until things cool off back in America. While he's there, Michael walks the streets of his Sicilian hometown, Corleone, with two bodyguards who are both carrying guns. He notices that hardly any men are walking the streets. "Where have all the men gone?" Michael asks his bodyguards. One responds, "They are all dead from vendettas." The three continue walking down the street, and Michael sees Apollonia for the first time and is impressed by her freshness and beauty. A bodyguard cautions Michael, "In Sicily, women are more dangerous than shotguns." Apparently Sicily at that time was a Wild West show with almost no governing laws. Danger was all around in the form of men and women alike, especially when it came to personal relationships.

The first person who told me that my father was killed was a family friend who looked into my family history for me when I was not quite ten years old. I was shocked. Over the years, I have buried the pain and disappointment of that revelation in a fantasy that my birth mother and father had a genuine, passionate, one-of-a-kind true love that you only read about in romance novels—a modern Romeo and Juliet. They were forbidden to see each other by their families, and like most things that are forbidden, their seeing each other became more enticing and exciting for this young, daring couple. They couldn't help but taste the forbidden fruit of their love, and nobody would stop their passion. I imagine that they met secretly in romantic places such as vast fields and beautiful gardens to consummate their relationship. I know it sounds like storybook imagery, but it's important for me to believe in this. I hold on to it to this day.

When I was five, my mother confirmed that I was adopted. While it was healthy for me to know this, I was somewhat abused by the other kids in my kindergarten class for being adopted. Eventually the teasing subsided, and by the second grade I found myself hanging out with the rich kids. I should never really have fit in with these kids, but somehow I mixed with them comfortably. I seemed to instinctively know etiquette. I knew how to behave in a nice home—places that smelled good and had expensive furnishings and attractive artwork. It seemed natural for me to be in that kind of environment, which was the complete opposite of how I felt in my house. This wasn't because I felt I deserved to be rich, but in my own home I felt like an outsider, never in the right place at the right time. We were poor—*really* poor.

Eleanor Roosevelt once said, "The future belongs to those who believe in the beauty of their dreams." I would often dream as a young child, and my dreams were vivid images of what I had hoped my life would actually be like growing up. I would dream that I was the belle of the ball, even royalty. In some of my dreams, I was surrounded by vast orchards chock-full of beautiful apples, grapes, and berries. The aromas I imagined were so pure, I thought they smelled the way heaven would. I played in green fields and ran free in these dreams. I skipped without a care in the world as the warm breezes blew through my hair. I was surrounded by family, and nobody seemed to ever have to work or worry. We ate amazing home-cooked meals and we all laughed, and I was an important part of that big, loving family. I would sit on my grandfather's lap and everyone would cherish and fawn over me. Everyone in these dreams didn't have distinct faces, but they always had bright smiles that were big, wide, and full of life. I was the only one in my dreams who had an actual face.

I would have these dreams almost every night. I suppose a lot of them were based on wishful thinking and my longing for the elements of a normal life that I missed out on as a kid, and every morning I was snapped back to my harsh reality. In my dreams I would be fed fresh fruit and expensive gourmet chocolates. In reality, for dinner, I would get frozen peas and a hockey puck for a hamburger that I would feed to the dog under the table. In my dreams I had a canopy bed. In reality my family moved around a lot, and in the less-than-humble homes I occupied as a child, rats were actually running around where I slept.

When I was thirteen years old, my mother told me more details surrounding my birth. She said that when she was at the hospital to pick me up and bring me home soon after I was born, she saw a young woman who was speaking Italian whom she believed to be my mother. Through the process of elimination she believes that it was, in fact, her. They passed each other in the hallway of the hospital and made eye contact. My mother looked curiously at my birth mother, who was being pushed in a wheelchair by an Italian woman who was thought to be my aunt. My aunt was tall, dark, and beautiful and was wearing her wedding band, which wasn't just any wedding band—it was covered in diamonds. My mother was extremely pretty, small-boned, and with a clear complexion and really long, curly hair.

I've been told I look exactly like my mother. I would joke and say, "Exactly *how* do I look like my mother?" I have never really thought I was attractive. I have always had a nice physique, but I've never liked my face. Maybe it's just hard for me to look in the mirror.

When you have been abused, as I was during my childhood,

it's hard to see yourself as the person whom everyone else sees on the surface. I thought it was best not to look in the mirror because of the reflection I saw from being abused. Despite it not being your fault, you feel guilty and dirty because of these painful and traumatic experiences. If someone liked something about me physically, I would immediately alter it. For instance, I had really long, curly hair just like my birth mother's. If someone liked my long hair, when I found this out, I went to a barbershop and got a boy's haircut because I didn't want anyone to look at me admiringly anymore. At forty-seven years old, when I look in the mirror, I see a much stronger woman than I have ever before seen. However, even now, I still don't see what the men who have loved me have seen in me. Maybe it's because I doubt whether they've actually seen my beauty on the inside. Or maybe I pushed them away before they were able to see it. I have a history of leaving men quickly because I am scared that when they get too close, they might actually get to know the real me. In hindsight, I think that's exactly what I wanted.

I believe that being given away by my mother at birth created a major sense of rejection that I have tried to overcome my entire life. Rejection can be a quick and simple act by one person to another, but reclaiming oneself after that rejection can be as daunting as climbing the world's highest mountain. To go through life is difficult in itself. But wondering about one's creation is serious grounds for insecurity and makes it more difficult to trust and love. However, it has been, and will continue to be, a journey that I will embrace and grow from.

The questions that run through the mind of a child who has been given up are many: *Who are my real parents? What are my roots? Where was I actually conceived?* The depth of insecurity that can result from this can only be imagined by most people. But I have known and lived with that insecurity every day of my life. My mother decided to give me away. She didn't want me. Even if she did want me, my grandfather took control and forced this young, weak woman to abandon me. The bottom line is that my whole family—my flesh and blood—did not want to include me in their lives. I think that this severe rejection made me easy prey for people in my life.

I have spent much of my life tapping into my own senses to try to discover some answers. I certainly had my share of childhood questions, and the answers weren't easy to come by. I had to dig in deep and try to piece together my story for myself as I daily learned more about who I was.

Some of the finer things in life that I now appreciate appear to have no connection whatsoever to any conscious experience I had during my childhood with my adoptive parents. My knowledge and appreciation of fine china, beautiful crystal, and the game of baccarat don't reflect any exposure to these that I had during my young life. I must have perceived these things when I was in the womb and exposed to my birth mother's upscale Italian family.

Flying in an airplane was another oddly familiar experience for me. I knew that first-class passengers boarded the plane before the other people even though I had never flown on an airplane before. Did it happen in this life when I was in my mother's womb flying to the United States for the first time? Or did it perhaps occur in another life? My friends have told me that they believe that all of this relates to some kind of special insight I have into the past. But I prefer to believe that it directly relates to my experiences as an unborn child in my mother's womb.

Another important part of my heritage that I think I picked up prior to my birth is Italian food. I can be in another room, smell an Italian dish cooking in the kitchen, and know precisely what is being prepared. Is this a coincidence? My answer is no. I believe that all of my knowledge of and appreciation for Italian food can be traced back to my Sicilian roots and the place where I was conceived. I was never formally taught how to cook Italian food. Yet today I know how to prepare sophisticated dishes without using any written recipes and instinctively know how to season the foods correctly as well.

The cliché is that Italians like to cook, eat, and reproduce. It's not surprising that those are among my favorite pastimes. (My mood and the company I am with determines where each item falls on my list.) I crave Italian food all the time. I imagine that I love to eat the things my birth mother ate when she was pregnant. Today, my daughters crave the same Italian foods that I ate when I was pregnant. I believe the child in her womb takes on his or her mother's tastes.

This may sound a little off-the-wall, but I think I absorbed my religious beliefs as well while in my mother's womb. I am close to my priest, Father Michael Lombardo of Our Lady of Consolation in Wayne, New Jersey, and consider my relationship with him special. I see Father Michael once a week. I have gone to church consistently throughout my life. My one stipulation to my parents as I grew up was that I had to be raised Catholic, even though I was living in a Protestant home. Luckily, I had friends who were Catholic, so I would go to mass with them and their families. I think my own children knew they were Catholic as soon as they were born. I blessed my belly all the time when I was pregnant.

When your family is a mystery that you wish to unravel and you desire answers to what might have been, you connect with your inner soul and senses more than other people usually do. You want to know where you came from. You want to find out how and why you think and feel the way you do. The questions of that journey don't stop there. It often takes years of denial before you have the strength to face certain problems, so you can't expect to resolve them overnight. At forty-seven years of age, I am still continuing to piece together my past and remain committed to my voyage of self-discovery. To learn is to live.

As a child, I spent every day of my life wondering if my birth mother would eventually contact me. Was she investigating *my* whereabouts and trying to seek me out? One thing's for certain:

I was constantly thinking about *her*. Was she thinking about me? Only she could answer that for sure, but as a mother, I know the deep emotional and spiritual connection that evolves from carrying a child. I can't imagine what it would be like to never be in contact with one of my daughters, so I doubt my mother just gave me up and forgot about me completely. But again, I may never know.

After my birth, I'm not sure exactly what happened to my mother next, except that she went back to Italy with my aunt. Over the years, friends have offered their assistance to help investigate her whereabouts for me. From what I have been told, my birth mother eventually settled right here in America. Further inquiries revealed that she eventually got married and that I'm now the oldest of six children. I know that if I chose to meet my mother and her new family, there would be extremely complicated issues and risks. For one thing, I'd be coming forward completely from left field as the oldest of all her children. Do I really want to alter my siblings' image of their mother by revealing that she gave birth to an illegitimate child? After forty-seven years have gone by, how does a sister announce to a brother she has never known, "Listen, I'm sorry to tell you this, but you weren't the first child born to our mother. I was." I've never wanted to destroy someone else's family unit, a group of innocent people who know nothing about me.

I convinced myself that my mom probably didn't come find me because she'd moved on and it would hurt her new family.

Or maybe they all did actually know about me but I was part of such a hurtful memory from the past that my mother was forbidden by her current husband to acknowledge it. Or maybe she just didn't care anymore. Of course, it could be a combination of all three. Or I could be completely wrong about all of these possibilities. One thing's for sure: I am quite curious.

Abortion was not an option for my birth mother for religious reasons, so her only choice was to eventually give me up for adoption. I admire her strength for coming all the way to the United States from Italy, giving birth to me, then walking away and believing that I would have a better life.

If my birth mother decided to come forward, I would like to speak with her. I'd like to find out why she never tried to find me after all these years. I would also like her to meet my children. I'd even like her to cook a meal with my daughters and me. It doesn't sound as if I'm asking for much, does it? Just an experience like what every daughter probably has with her mother. As a mom, I cook with my daughters often, and it's always time well spent together—we share ideas and thoughts and talk about our lives and dreams. We make dishes together from start to finish, enjoy our accomplishments, and savor the taste of food cooked with love. I realize that this might sound simple, but I think these moments are extremely important to our development as women.

I've spent a good part of my life wondering what the conversation would be like between my birth mother and me if we ever met one-on-one. All she would have to do is look me in the eye and say, "I'm sorry." It seems like such a simple gesture. I would just want her to say something that would make me truly believe in my heart and soul that she feels bad that I had to go through even a minute of what I endured during my childhood. Once my birth mother offered me a heartfelt apology, I wouldn't discuss the subject with her again. Not ever again.

2

STOLEN FLOWER

was five days old when my parents picked me up at the hospital in the summer of 1962. I was a big healthy baby with a full head of tight brown ringlets. My mother said my birth mother must have had a lot of agita during her pregnancy because that's what happens to mothers who give birth to babies with a lot of hair. She also said that I was the most beautiful baby in the nursery and she was so happy to get me. They named me Beverly.

When I arrived home with my new parents, they had playthings suited only for boys. They'd had six boys prior to my arrival and didn't know if they would be adopting a boy or a girl, so they weren't prepared for a female. They didn't care if I was a boy or a girl, just as long as they got a healthy baby. However, it seemed that my mother didn't quite know how to take care of a completely healthy baby. I suppose that's understandable, since her own sons had all been seriously ill.

My parents were struggling with the trauma of having lost five of their birth children to cystic fibrosis. At the time I entered their lives, they were trying to keep the sixth one, Ronnie, alive and were making frequent trips back and forth to the Children's Hospital for Cystic Fibrosis in Philadelphia.

Cystic fibrosis is a chronic, life-threatening disease that impairs the lungs' capacity to hold enough air for normal breathing on one's own. A thick mucus forms in the lungs and digestive tract, creating a blockage. This inherited disease strikes children and young adults. Some treatments and various oxygen tanks have been specially designed to combat it, but it's a pretty tough illness to live with.

I was told that as sick as he was, when Ronnie first saw me, he couldn't take his eyes off me. He would say, "Mommy, she has the biggest brown eyes I've ever seen," and he seemed fascinated that he now had a baby sister. I was adopted when Ronnie was seven, and I spent approximately two years with him before he died. I know that he adored me; just having me around seemed to generate a great deal of happiness for him. I don't think Ronnie realized how sick he really was because he always seemed so full of life. He had a zest for life undaunted by his disease, and it certainly did not affect his quality of life except temporarily when he was taken for his treatments to the Philadelphia hospital twice a week. I am not quite sure if it was more for Ronnie's sake or my parents' sake that I was adopted, but after Ronnie was born and diagnosed the doctor had advised my mother and father to stop having children because their genetics didn't properly mesh.

I've been told that at the time my father seemed to be happy on the surface, but a distinct sadness was behind his eyes. He'd lost five sons and knew that Ronnie was soon going to die. I think I was a breath of fresh air for my mother, amid all of the pain of loss and dealing with Ronnie's illness. Compared to Ronnie, I was easy to take care of. She didn't have to drive me to the hospital for oxygen or put me on medication. I was never sick. I know my mother loves me to this day, but I was always aware that I had to be independent and cause minimal trouble for her because as a mom she was already stretched too thin.

One day, I tried to wake Ronnie from his nap, the way I normally did, by climbing up on the couch and giving him a big hug. I would never lie on his chest though—I would carefully put my head next to his, put my nose gently in his neck, and nuzzle him to wake him up. He didn't move. I was young and confused, and at first I thought he was playing a game, but I didn't find it funny. I was scared. Ronnie never woke up that afternoon.

That was the first time someone I loved had died, and I was just two years old. Ronnie had lived to be nine, then the darkness set in and the dynamic completely changed at my parents' house soon after he passed away.

After Ronnie's death, my family attempted to have a normal life. We lived in the small town of Athens, Pennsylvania, which was about three hours from Philadelphia and had one stoplight. Our house was close to the school where I attended kindergarten, and I spent a great deal of time alone, but didn't mind. I would come home from kindergarten to an empty house because both my parents were working. I actually liked being alone when I came home. It was the nicest house we had ever lived in, with hardwood floors, cathedral ceilings, gorgeous moldings, and spacious bay windows. The kitchen was huge, with almost pantry-size cabinets. After school I would climb up on the countertops and get treats such as Suzy Q's, Yodels, and Twinkies from the oversize cabinets. At the time, my mother was an insurance broker and my father was a minister and also sold real estate. We were doing pretty well, but this period of success lasted only a short time.

Since my father was a minister, people frequently came to our home for counseling. It seemed that the bulk of them were women. Rumor had it that he was having affairs with several of them. My father was lost after Ronnie died. I think he needed to feel a new kind of love and wasn't sure what it was supposed to consist of. The women were seeking guidance, and maybe my father took a little advantage of that. My mom told me years later that this is why he was asked to leave the ministry, and we had to move out of the town we lived in.

From then on, it seemed that our family was always really poor. Everything I owned was a hand-me-down. When I was quite young, I would go to the local supermarket alone and thumb through fashion magazines such as *Vogue* and *Cosmopolitan* and imagine what it would be like to own some beautiful dresses like the ones within their pages. While I dreamed of wearing fabulous and fashionable clothes, the fantasy and my life couldn't have been further apart.

Sexual abuse entered my life when I was extremely young. I would go to bed thinking that it should be a time when I could just go to sleep. But bedtime for me was different from the way most children are able to go to sleep. I would lie in bed and worry if this night would be a repeat of other nights prior. Then my bedroom door would quietly open in the middle of the night at different times and in would come a relative or family friend—one of my abusers—who'd climb into bed with me and treat me with no regard. I was a little girl, scared to death and in so much pain from what they were doing to me. The creak from that door slowly opening still haunts me to this day. I eventually gave up fighting the advances. I just let it happen to me, submitting to the abuse.

As soon as the door opened, my dog, Suzie, would immediately jump from my arms, off the bed, and hide underneath, cringing in fright. I would bury my head in my pillow and tightly grip the side of the mattress with one hand while my other hand would hang off the side of the bed so that my puppy could lick it from below. It helped us to comfort each other. Suzie and I were both scared.

I guess that I eventually became numb to the abuse. Can you imagine what it feels like to be tied down, but you don't actually have restraints on you? That was exactly how I felt when I was being touched. I felt completely helpless, as if I were paralyzed. I could only imagine my abusers justifying these sick scenes to themselves and saying, "Well, I didn't have to tie her down." Of course they didn't have to tie me down. They were violating a child!

I remember when my dreams as a child turned from hopeful and happy to extremely dark after the abuse started. In fact, I no longer had dreams. Now, they were always nightmares. In my dreams prior, there were vast orchards filled with apples and berries where I played hide-and-seek and ran through freely. Now they were just dead fields. The friendly dream figures that once bore only bright, big smiles were now distinct with recognizable faces—the faces of my abusers. I could clearly hear them and see them, and it was scary. There were only broken branches on the barren ground and nowhere to hide. I was completely exposed and easy prey. As a young child, I couldn't find sanctuary, not even in my dreams.

The psychological damage to me as a child was unimaginable. I would go to school the day after being sexually abused bleeding from my crotch because I'd scrubbed my privates in the shower that morning with Brillo. I'd scrubbed and scrubbed, trying in desperation to remove the sense of shame and the evil smell of them from me. I remember taking a wooden spoon and scraping my insides clean. No matter how hard I tried, I couldn't get rid of the dirty and repulsive feeling of their being inside me.

I loved Barbie dolls as a kid. Early on, before the abuse started, my Barbie dolls were dressed beautifully and had flowing hair. Later, in the midst of the horror show of abuse, I cut their hair off and covered their butts and private areas with Vaseline. I must have covered my dolls' private areas with Vaseline because that's what these men used.

I have been asked why I never tried to run away from home. Honestly, I thought I had nowhere to run to because I assumed that this kind of sexual abuse was happening to kids everywhere. I was so naive that I didn't know how to define what was happening to me, much less label it as "sexual abuse." At that point in my life I was still very young.

Little did I know, while most kids had members of their families singing lullabies to help them fall asleep, I was being told to hush up and be quiet so that no one would hear my cries.

———

With no hope for a change in reality, I resorted to a coping mechanism that has carried me through for far longer than most people maintain relationships with imaginary friends. I am not exactly sure when Nicky first came into my life, but

I think she might've first appeared when Ronnie died. Since then, she has always been there for me.

I invented Nicky when I was a young child, and her appearance seemed natural to me. When I was in kindergarten, I got into a lot of trouble for making up Nicky. My teacher said, "Nicky is not here and doesn't really exist. You need to stop scaring the other kids." In all innocence I replied, "I'm not trying to scare anyone. Nicky is here to make sure that I'm not scared."

Nicky was usually standing right next to me as a child, holding my hand tightly and guiding me through life. Nicky was the opposite of me. She had blond hair and blue eyes. I have brown hair and brown eyes. She was happy when I was sad. She had no fear and I was afraid of everything. She was strong and I was weak. She pushed herself and I didn't. She was aggressive and I wasn't. She was a fighter and I was more of a lover. Nicky didn't care if she was accepted, when all I ever wanted was to be accepted. She was really beautiful and I wasn't. Nicky was never judged, and I was judged all the time. Nicky was never misunderstood while I was completely misunderstood. She was the girl next door and I was the girl nobody wanted to live next door to. Nicky was everything I wished I was and couldn't be. The exception was that Nicky could never and I could always cook really well. That was pretty much the only advantage I had over her. Nicky was always talking to me and encouraging me. She would continually tell me that I was sweet and pretty, and she had the amazing ability to dispel negativity. She would say to me, "You don't have to hate those people who are against you. I'll hate them for you." Nicky would also never let me take the blame for anything. She always accepted responsibility and tried to leave me feeling no guilt whatsoever. For instance, when I was sixteen years old, my dad and mom went away for the weekend. My dad had recently bought a brand-new truck, which I decided to take for a joyride to get a milk shake and fries. I had only a learner's permit and didn't realize how difficult it would be to drive a big truck across a small bridge. The truck had huge side mirrors mounted on long extensions. I was driving across the small bridge quickly, and at the end of the bridge, the road sharply veered off to the right. I was not an experienced enough driver to successfully make the turn and ripped the chrome and the mirror right off the side of my father's brand-new truck.

I pulled over to the side of the road and sat there in shock. Nervously I asked, "Nicky, what the hell am I going to do now?" She immediately suggested that I go to the house of my friend Lisa, who had just gotten a driver's license. Nicky said we should ask Lisa to go for a ride in the truck, but we shouldn't let her see the side of the truck that was damaged. She told me that Lisa could be blamed for the accident.

I pulled up to Lisa's house, turned off the engine, and then realized, *Wait a minute. Nicky is not going to be able to ask Lisa to go out with me for a ride. I will have to do the asking. I can't do that. She'll see right through me.* I did end up asking Lisa to go for a ride, but unexpectedly she walked over to get inside from the damaged side of the truck. Surprised, Lisa asked, "What did you do?" I looked her straight in the eye and told her that I had screwed up my dad's truck on the bridge. Lisa saw how afraid I was and immediately offered to loan me the money to get the truck repaired. It was $120 to get the truck fixed—that was a lot of money at the time.

A part of me enjoyed the attention I derived from wrecking my dad's truck. While I got it fixed, when my dad came home, I still admitted what I had done. Surprisingly, my father didn't do anything except give me the money to return to Lisa.

Nicky did not always offer the best advice, but she did always provide me with good company, and I believe Nicky was an important key to my maintaining my sanity when I was being sexually abused. Besides my puppy, Suzie, I had only her to talk to about it, and sometimes I could feel Nicky touching my hair the way I wished my mother would. At other times she'd tell me that what my abusers did was wrong, and she was sorry she wasn't strong enough to keep them away from me. Nicky always wanted to fight for me. She just wasn't physically big enough to fend anybody off. She felt somewhat guilty that she couldn't prevent what was happening. She could only be there and support me through it. She was present when I needed her, and that was all that really mattered.

Gradually, in high school, I became much more confident as I came into my own and I needed less and less of Nicky. These days she appears infrequently, but it's reassuring to know that she's still available if I have to call upon her; Nicky still comes around when I *really* need her.

I am aware that Nicky doesn't exist outside of my own mind. I gave her life because she helped me with mine, and I know that without her I couldn't have survived many of the tragic things that happened to me as a child. At times I'd actually convince myself that the abuse was happening to Nicky and not to me. Sometimes, when you are falling through the cracks in life, there's no safety net. But I always had Nicky.

3

BRIGHT LIGHTS
IN A DARK WORLD

My aunt Barbara was one of the strongest blessings in my childhood. From early on, she said proudly to my mom, "Watch out for that one. There's something very special about that little girl."

Aunt Barbara and her husband, Uncle Bob, were a breath of fresh air, *literally*. As opposed to my immediate family, they always smelled good. I couldn't wait to see my aunt, hug her, and breathe her in—she always wore the latest and most expensive perfume and couture designs. Uncle Bob would smoke a pipe filled with cherry tobacco that smelled delicious. I always felt safe and content when they were around. My aunt and uncle owned several beautiful homes in Manhattan, Toronto, and California. I don't remember what they did for a living—it wasn't important to me. My aunt Barbara was my mom's sister. The youngest of nine children, she was very different from the rest of her family, so much more worldly and well traveled than all the others. She and her husband obviously knew about the finer things in life. I don't know why I was so drawn to them. Maybe it was because of the money and their ability to buy the better things, stuff I wasn't accustomed to, or perhaps it was just because they actually treated me like a little girl . . . a little princess, in fact. The way they treated me was a bright light in contrast to the darkness of my life at home with my parents.

Unfortunately, Aunt Barb (as I liked to call her) wasn't a daily presence in my life; she visited only on holidays and when we had special family events. She and Uncle Bob *became* my Christmas. They would show up at our home in the latest and most expensive new Cadillac. Where I came from, it was always a big deal to have a luxury car, and when she would arrive, it felt like a red-carpet event. Barbara was tan and pretty and her hair was always perfectly highlighted. Her skin was amazing, beautiful, bronzed, and glowing. Best of all, when I looked into her kind eyes, I could tell she was genuinely happy to see me. She would always make a big deal about my doing cartwheels and splits, and when I played my flute, she was transfixed until I finished the last note of the song.

When Aunt Barbara was around, I felt that no one would dare misbehave or abuse me in any way. I was sure that she and my uncle Bob would easily pick up on something like that.

Therefore, every fiber of my being felt at ease when I was in her company.

When I was fifteen years old, Aunt Barbara became ill with cancer. I was devastated, but I thought that even though she was sick, she wouldn't die. *She is going to be in my life forever,* I thought.

My mother went to visit Barbara in California for three weeks while she was ill. With my mom away, my father went off somewhere, so nobody was home watching me. I had a boyfriend at the time, but he was away at college. My appendix ruptured when I was by myself. I was so sick that I could barely move. I tried to get to the phone, which was mounted on the wall in the kitchen, to call for help, but was so weak that I could barely stand up. I yanked the phone off the wall in desperation, then passed out on the kitchen floor.

My boyfriend drove home from college that day, and twelve hours later he found me, still lying on the floor unconscious. He rushed me to the hospital, where the doctors did an emergency appendectomy (I have a scar that goes from my pubic bone all the way up to my belly button from the surgery). My mother finally arrived from California and rushed to the hospital to check on me. I was still weak and had lost twenty pounds when she arrived, but I could hear a lot of yelling out in the hallway— my mother was extremely upset because my father hadn't been there for me. When my mother came into my hospital room to comfort me, all I wanted to know was how Aunt Barbara was doing. I could not have cared less about myself.

Not long after, I saw Aunt Barbara when she made a visit to the East Coast. Sadly, it was one of her last—she was obviously losing her battle with cancer. She was weak, and I knew she didn't have long to live. As we talked, she started saying she was sorry; she was sorry because she had to die and leave me. I asked her not to go. Begged her. I was heartbroken. When she passed away, I was very aware that no one else in the world believed in me the way she had, and I suddenly felt incredibly alone and truly lost without her. It was also clear to me that I wouldn't feel safe around my family ever again.

At Aunt Barbara's funeral, I lay across the top of her casket, sobbing and not wanting to leave her. I didn't want them to close the top of the coffin because I didn't want to ever stop seeing her face. People kept coming up to me and telling me we had to leave the funeral home; Uncle Bob was the only one who could comfort me and get me to let go. For some reason, I never again saw Uncle Bob after that day, but whenever I smell cherry tobacco, I can't help but think of him. Those are some of the best memories.

———

I was upset for a long time after Aunt Barbara's death. I questioned God. I didn't understand why this woman who had been so incredibly kind to me was taken away so soon. First Ronnie, then Barbara—why did the people who loved me die?

I don't have many good memories after my aunt Barbara's

death, except for those of my horse, Love (this was a different era, and horses were cheap to buy in the country in those days). She was beautiful, lean and tall, with a black mane, tail, and forelock, and a chestnut brown body. To me, horses represented freedom and I always felt more in control when I was in their presence.

I knew how to ride horses well. I rode western mostly, but I was also trained in equestrian-style riding, which I thought felt too formal. Love was an incredible show horse. She jumped well and did the obstacle course perfectly. She could turn on a dime and pirouette like a ballerina. She was incredibly fast. Love would put her head back, take off, and just go and go! I think she needed to let loose and run just as I did. I would lie on her neck and the horse would practically fly. She would run so hard that she'd have foam coming out of her mouth. I didn't have to kick or use spurs or a riding crop: all I would have to do was hold on. We had a unique bond and trusted each other fully. And *nobody* could get on that horse but me.

My father owned a stallion, named Diablo, that he kept in upstate New York along with Love. This was another horse nobody could ride but me. My father would attempt to ride Diablo, but the horse would behave wildly as soon as he climbed on his back. Diablo would try to turn and bite my father's ankle in an attempt to get him off. I would always chuckle to myself watching Diablo try to shake off my father. Then I would mount Diablo and he would be completely relaxed and at ease. Diablo ran fast, too.

I began to show my horse, Love, a lot more as I took up

competitive western horseback riding. I'd compete every week-end and became very good friends with Susan, whom I met at the horse shows. I eventually spent a lot of time at her family's gorgeous ranch in upstate New York. They had huge stables that were cleaner than most people's homes! One day Susan told me that her brother Luke had a crush on me. In fact, Luke was the first boy who took interest in me. He was a great horse-back rider and I had an instant connection with him. It was an innocent flirtation. We didn't do anything beyond hold hands and have nice conversations. I couldn't wait for the weekends so I could ride horses and see Luke.

The few things that I enjoyed in my childhood eventually somehow fell apart, and one night my father didn't close the corral gate correctly and Love escaped. She reached the high-way and was hit by a truck and killed. I was inconsolable. Love was not only my pride and joy, but also my friend. Heartbroken after the loss of my horse, I lost contact with Luke and Susan. What a shock to lose her in this way—the one thing left in my young life that I truly loved.

—————

When I was eight years old, my father decided that he wanted to foster another child. My parents didn't want a baby, as it would have been a lot of responsibility. They wanted a boy or girl who was a bit older. We had fostered many children during the years after my arrival, and in the end, my parents never opted to adopt any of them, with one exception—Pam.

Pam was a year older than me when she came to our home. I remember that she was a sad child who had seemingly survived quite a bit before becoming a part of our family. When one sad person looks into the sad eyes of another, you can almost imagine what they have been through in their life. I find that this particular level of sadness often can be a common thread between two lost people.

Soon after Pam arrived, the sexual abuse slowed down quite a bit and eventually came to a halt before my ninth birthday. I believe that my abusers felt Pam would tell on them. We shared my bedroom and now what had been my personal space was occupied by more than just myself. This prevented me from remaining easy prey.

Now, just because the abuse physically stopped, it didn't mean that what had taken place hadn't scarred me. Wonderful innocence had been completely stolen from me, as had the beautiful discovery of what intimacy could be. I've had to redefine intimacy over the past forty-seven years without truly being able to discover it for the first time through love.

By the age of eight, I had already been severely sexually abused. I had gone through far too much for any eight-year-old to endure. I was too young to know wrong or right in the moral sense, but I did know that it didn't feel good. In those days, nobody spoke about sexual abuse openly the way they do now. I was made to believe that if I told anybody, I was disposable—that I would no longer be of use. I thought that I would be considered damaged and my parents would give me up for adoption again. So I just kept my mouth shut about the abuse and held it inside, which became my own personal battle.

It turns out that my mother didn't know until I told her when I was in my late twenties. Mind you, I wasn't telling my mother about the abuse in an accusing fashion. I was telling her about it because I finally got to the point where I *could* tell her and felt compelled to share. I had gone through rehab, counseling, and therapy. The sexual abuse from my childhood was one of the issues that I needed to confront and try to put to rest. Telling my mom about it was an important first step in that process.

Immediately after I told my mother, she sat in a state of shock. For a few moments, she stared blankly and her skin became very pale. It seemed as though she wasn't even exhaling. It wasn't as if she didn't believe me—she was in a state of total confusion. *How could I have not known about this? How could you have gone all of these years without telling me?* she must have thought. When she tried to stand, she actually fell to her knees on the kitchen floor. She was wiped out emotionally—exhausted from processing all of this in her head.

4

BILLY THE KID

When I was thirteen years old, I began to notice boys. One that stood out from the rest was Peter, who was a few years older than me. I admired him from afar, gazing at him through a fence at our local playground. He was really cute—built well, with dark hair, big brown eyes, a great smile with perfect teeth, and dimples. All the girls in my school had a crush on Peter, and he always seemed to have a girlfriend. One after another wore his class ring, which was unique because it was pink amethyst (his birthstone).

His array of female fans included popular cheerleaders who were rich, pretty, and came from perfect families—they were all the things I wasn't. However, Peter and I eventually connected when he came to work for my father one summer doing odd jobs. We saw each other every day and became extremely close, and by summer's end we were in love. My crush from afar became my boyfriend. The class ring that was once worn by so many girls I envied was now on *my* finger. It felt like a fairy tale. Peter was the first guy I had true feelings for. He was the first guy I experienced love with. He was my first willing sexual experience. He was my first everything.

We got engaged when I was fifteen years old. After six months together, right before his senior prom, Peter gave me a diamond ring and asked me to marry him. I said yes, of course, and after our amazing summer together, Peter went off to a college that was four hours away. We wrote to each other often and I talked to him on the phone every night. I baked him chocolate chip cookies every Tuesday and mailed them to him on Wednesday. We were so much in love that it was sickening.

Then, all of a sudden, I wasn't in love anymore.

Soon after Peter went away to college, I felt as if something was missing. I wanted to get out of the relationship with him, but didn't know how. After all, he was my fiancé. I didn't know how to end a relationship, so I did the only thing that I was taught up to that point. . . . I cheated on him by hooking up with my girlfriend's brother. My father had cheated on my mother throughout my entire childhood, and cheating was my only reality. Children do learn what they live.

When my father found out that I had cheated on Peter, he yelled at me. I was completely shocked that he had a problem with it. "You didn't teach me how to love," I yelled at him. "You didn't teach me what a normal relationship was supposed to feel like. You cheated on Mom while I babysat the children of your mistress! Now *you* have a problem with me cheating on Peter?"

I eventually told Peter that I wasn't interested in being with him anymore. He was devastated. Peter was still as in love with me as I had been with him in the sixth and seventh grade, when I'd gazed at him from afar and dreamed of what it would be like to call him mine. I broke up with Peter in the kitchen of my house and literally stepped over him as I walked out the front door. I will never forget the look on his face. I deeply hurt him. He was a good guy and didn't deserve it. However, I didn't see it that way back then. The more Peter cried about our breakup, the angrier I got. As tears rolled down Peter's cheeks, his anguish fed the rage I felt toward my abusers and what they'd done to me as a child. I was emotionally abusing Peter for what they did to me. By breaking Peter's heart, it somehow made me feel vindicated for the pain of my childhood. Little did I know I'd go on to do this to other men throughout my life.

After my breakup with Peter, I discovered that a lot of guys really wanted to be with me. This realization fed the feminine beast inside me even more. I was sixteen years old and finally coming into my own. I guess I was a late bloomer; prior to that time I was tall and lanky and had no breasts. "Hey, Olive Oyl, where's your Popeye?" the boys and girls would mock me. But suddenly there was no more Olive Oyl, and the boys definitely started to take notice.

My long legs suddenly took shape. My breasts, albeit small, were developing and my skinny waistline began to give proportion to my body. I began to walk differently—sexier, and with a lot more confidence. I had beautiful, long, brown curly hair that complemented my bone structure.

Because I was extremely poor and not very outgoing, I'd had trouble fitting in. Now things began to change for me for the better. I started to make some money from cleaning houses and babysitting, which allowed me to buy some new clothes and wear outfits that were in style. I bought a pair of tight designer jeans that fit me well, and people started to look at me differently. I used a hair conditioner that was top of the line that made my hair full and silky, and I got noticed. I learned a lot about accentuating my outer beauty as I matured, and how to take advantage of it. Without a doubt, going into my early teens was a difficult transitional time for me. However, I successfully came out the other side with many male suitors in tow, one of whom was extremely important: Billy.

I met Billy at a bar in upstate New York when I was seventeen years old. A lot of bands played at this big, two-story club—*the* local place for loud rock music and a rowdy crowd fueled on beers and shots. When I think of that place, I'm immediately reminded of the movie *Road House* starring Patrick Swayze.

I had a job, and the first thing I wanted to do was move out of my house. My friend Tammy was not happy at home either.

We had met in high school and decided to become roommates. We would go out often to dance. It was a way for both of us to relieve the stresses in our lives. She was a pretty brunette with a really nice physique, but a bit depressed. She was a fun girl with guy problems, something that plagued Tammy and me and most other girls in their teens.

Tammy was eighteen, which was the legal drinking age at the time. I usually got into bars because I was almost the legal age, though having a fake ID and fluttering my long lashes at the bouncer helped my cause as well. There wasn't as much of a hassle back then as there is today about underage drinking. It was a fun time to be a young girl emerging out of her teens.

The bartender, Craig, had been serving me a lot of kamikaze shots on the night Billy and I met. I was only seventeen but could pound shots back. Not long after I arrived at the club, I spotted Billy from across the bar. We made eye contact and there was an immediate connection. We mouthed a hello to each other and he came over and bought me a drink. He was attractive—half-Italian and half-Irish, with *GQ* looks and a body like a brick shithouse. But even though our eyes met like two magnets, I didn't approach him. I never approached guys—I still don't to this day. I have never found it necessary to approach men ... though maybe that's been my problem: throughout my life the wrong ones have always approached me.

Billy asked me if I would like to dance. When we hit the

dance floor, Craig's eyes were on us like lasers burning holes into our backs. He had a massive crush on me and was protective. Craig would always make sure to walk me safely to my car from the club at the end of the night, and he would even follow me and my friends home. However, despite Craig's attention, Billy and I danced all night. It was pretty much love at first sight.

From that night on, Billy and I were inseparable. We were young and in love, the type of love that was as pure as the driven snow. I wanted to be with him all the time, and Billy was so proud of me that he introduced me to everybody he had ever known. He also loved to take photographs of me. He took beautiful shots of me in Central Park surrounded by colorful foliage in bright Indian-summer sunshine.

Billy and I dated during an era of free love. There was no AIDS scare, and unprotected sex just meant that you could get pregnant. However, I still practiced safe sex. I was an adopted child and my mother was young when she got pregnant, so to me, safe sex was a choice I made for myself. Besides, guys always carried condoms back in those days, even in the midst of the free love movement. I don't know if that's still the case today. I don't mean to disappoint anyone, but I am not out there banging everything that walks. Even back then I wasn't having sex with multiple partners. I enjoyed being in a relationship. And Billy and I were in a committed relationship.

When I met him, Billy was a police officer who was also studying law in New York City. When Billy would go to the city to attend classes, Craig would consistently come around and try to keep me company. He would show up at my house and profess his love. Even though I'd never even so much as kissed Craig, he was determined to spend the rest of his life with me. One night he said to me, "If I asked you to marry me, what would you say?"

I replied, "I would have to say no." I was always up front about how I felt about him.

Craig was genuine about his feelings, too. He had plenty of opportunities to take advantage of me when I was drunk, but he never did. While he wasn't *GQ* material the way Billy was, he definitely had a swagger about him and a nice build. A lot of pretty girls were chasing after him. I suppose I misled Craig, but I did it innocently. I was too young to realize what was really going on. Looking back now, I know it wasn't a good idea to string Craig along. However, I wasn't doing it intentionally. I just selfishly needed the kind of attention he gave me. Craig made me feel safe when Billy wasn't around. He also made Billy jealous, and I needed that as well.

Billy was fully aware that Craig was actively pursuing me, and one night things almost got out of hand. Unexpectedly, Billy came back from New York City early to surprise me and arrived at my house the same time as Craig. Billy walked up to Craig as he approached my front door and grabbed his arm from behind. From the window I saw they were having a verbal altercation that looked to be moments away from getting physical.

I heard Billy say, "I appreciate you watching out for her when I'm not around, but this is getting out of hand. Take my advice and walk away with dignity."

Well, Craig didn't want to walk away. He was willing to fight for me. However, Billy decided that he had already won and refused to take the bait. Eager to defuse the situation, I went outside and immediately asked Craig to leave. He was obviously hurt, and that was the last time I ever saw him.

Over the next couple of months, Billy and I drove back and forth to Florida, trying to decide whether we wanted to move down there permanently or not. Billy wanted to quit the police because he was sick of arresting people for laws that he didn't believe in. For example, he felt smoking pot should be legal, and he didn't like arresting people, confiscating their drugs, then watching the goods being distributed among his fellow officers. He felt the whole thing was hypocritical and didn't believe in his line of work anymore. He dreamed of being a musician and wanted to pursue it, and Florida seemed at the time like the place to do that.

Billy was quite a good musician. He played acoustic guitar and sang James Taylor—Jimmy Buffet–style. The lyrics in the songs were about love, struggle, family, and heartache. I believed Billy could have been the next James Taylor.

Once Billy quit his job, we didn't really keep a regular schedule. We'd stay up till all hours talking to each other, sharing stories and private details about our lives. Billy's experience in law enforcement and his training in how to investigate people led him to believe that something was going on beneath the surface with me, and it was clear to him that I was hiding something important about my life. Well, that something was my sordid past of sexual abuse during my childhood. One night while we were visiting upstate New York, Billy got me to open up and I told him everything about that dark part of my life.

My dad was the only father that I have ever known. With that said, I harbored anger toward him my entire life for failing to protect me. It came to a boiling point when I finally opened up for the first time to Billy. Having that come out of me all at once made me realize that Nicky had been handling a lot all by herself and she didn't have to any longer. I could tell by Billy's expression that Nicky was in good company. I know now what I didn't know then—when my father adopted me, he signed on to protect, love, and cherish me. And above all, his obligation was to never allow anyone to lay one single finger on me. I often wondered why my father adopted me in the first place if he knew that he would not be capable of loving me as if I were his own child. He failed miserably. Nicky noticed it and now Billy did, too.

I don't know what made me tell him everything, but it felt right. Afterward, he looked me straight in the eyes and said, "Let's go."

I didn't have to ask where we were going. I just knew.

We immediately got into Billy's little Toyota and drove to the nearby town where my father had been living since my parents' divorce. It was cold and icy when we pulled up to my father's girlfriend's house. Billy was usually an easygoing, happy guy, never without a smile or handshake for whomever he met. However, as soon as Billy got out of the car, he had a crazy look in his eyes that let me know that this visit was not going to go well.

The small house had a garage and a carport that you could pull under. Billy approached the house and banged on the screen door at the side entrance by the carport. My dad answered the door in good spirits.

Without hesitation, Billy grabbed my father by the back of his sweater and pulled him out of the doorway. He threw my dad down on the grass next to the carport.

Although my father deserved something for failing to prevent the abuse, I found it difficult to watch since I am not a violent person. This all felt wrong to me so I turned away. I believe two wrongs never make a right. While the beating continued, I stayed in the fetal position in the car, facing the other direction. Billy was in really good shape—Marine Corps–caliber shape. My dad had heart problems and had recently had a fifth bypass. Truthfully, I became concerned.

I beeped the horn and yelled out the car window, "Billy, stop! That's enough! Let's go!" My father was lying on the ground crying. For a brief moment, I actually felt bad for him, but mainly I was afraid Billy would go to prison and then be removed from my life like everyone else I loved.

At last Billy got into the car, looked me in the eyes, and said, "You deserve to be loved and feel safe, and I'm sorry if watching that hurt you. But no one has ever protected you as your father should have. This is a new start for you. I'm here for you now and I will keep you safe."

I've never had someone in my life willing to protect and defend me the way Billy did. I guess that protective streak only comes when you truly love someone. My father never pressed charges against Billy. Perhaps it was because of a certain level of guilt he felt about my childhood. Or maybe it was the era. Nobody sued in those days. I'll never really know for sure. Either way, we didn't hear from him after the incident.

The next day, Billy and I went back to Florida for good. Nobody could stop us.

———————

Billy and I drove down to Florida in thirty hours straight. Billy did the majority of the driving, and we talked almost the entire time. We felt as if we were returning to Florida for real.

When Billy and I got to Florida, the roommates he usually crashed with down there were less than thrilled to now have a woman living in their house full-time. It was supposed to be a bachelor pad. Soon after, Billy and I moved out.

We were homeless and slept in the Toyota packed to the brim with all of our personal belongings. We parked the car at the beach at night and fell asleep to the sounds of the ocean. At sunrise we'd wake up and use the public-beach showers. It seemed like a bit of an adventure at first, but we soon realized that we couldn't live on love alone forever. We were hungry and tired. Real life was starting to take its toll. So we hit the pavement, trying to find work, and within a short time I landed a few waitressing jobs. Within six weeks we moved into a small apartment right on the ocean in Pompano Beach, a popular community north of Fort Lauderdale.

I was working three waitressing jobs while Billy bartended, and we both decided to model to bring in extra cash. Billy was modeling when he lived in New York City, and I had been approached by scouts back then as well. I was referred to a modeling agency in Florida and went in for a meeting. The agency loved me but didn't love my hair, which was really long—down to my bottom—stringy, and curly. These days, it's fashionable to have naturally curly hair, but not back then. The fashion powers that be also said that my eyebrows had to be shaped and I needed to learn how to wear makeup. They sent me to a talented makeover specialist named Tommy DeRosa, who immediately became my first gay love. He was funny and good-looking, and we laughed and talked freely about everything as if we had known each other our whole lives. I knew a lot of gay guys back then in Miami, but I didn't love any of the others as much as Tommy. Spending time with him was a blast; it also made me realize I'd always feel safe being around gay men, since I felt that I could let my guard down in a way I wasn't used to doing around straight men.

Tommy made me over and my curls ended up looking perfect—
my look was updated to what people wanted in the eighties.
The agency loved it and immediately started sending me on
go-sees for swimsuit-catalog modeling and leg modeling.

Billy and I were young, hustling, and doing quite well. In
the early eighties, cash was easy to make in Florida. Plus, most
of the jobs that were offered enabled you to party while you
worked. You got the best of both worlds. In those days, Florida
was one big party. It was like having spring break all year long.
They say that New York City is the city that never sleeps. Well,
Florida doesn't sleep, either, especially in the Miami and Fort
Lauderdale areas, where doing drugs and partying is the local
pastime.

Billy and I eventually moved into a small but nice "rent
to buy" home in Fort Lauderdale. We were working a lot and
making good money, and we were homeowners in no time.

Over the next few years in Florida, it was work hard, play
hard . . . We even played hard at work. I was using a lot of speed.
I worked at four bars, clocking in ninety to a hundred hours a
week, and I was *speeding* through it. Everybody in the restaurant business in the early eighties was doing speed. Nobody
could even sell it to anybody else because everyone had his or
her own stock. You could order the stuff through the mail from
magazines.

One of the bars I worked at was a five-star place called
September's, a big hangout for Florida fat cats. The section I
worked in saw the most action and was always packed. My sales

were consistently at the top. It was mind-boggling how many drinks I could sell in one night. I even sold more drinks than the blond waitress who was banging the manager. I was just good at what I did. The uniforms at September's were kind of like Playboy Bunny outfits—they were miniversions of tuxedos, all in black and white. The outfit was a primarily a black leotard that was cut high over the hip, and we wore black tights underneath. The top of the leotard was scooped low around the chest, then went up over the shoulders and was cut even lower in the back as well. The scoops were trimmed in white dress-shirt ruffle. The leotard was topped off by a thick red cummerbund and a red bow tie. We also wore a tuxedo cuff on each arm, and black high heels—the higher the better. The outfit appealed to the customers, as you can imagine.

September's had one of the most exclusive VIP rooms in all of Fort Lauderdale. I was selling some bottles that cost as much as $8,000 and getting tipped to open them, serve them, taste them, and sometimes share them with the customers. Florida had a lot of excess money at that time. Not only was I making money, I was also making connections with some of the wealthiest and most powerful people in Florida.

The more loyal clientele you built up, the better money you made. I had a great, extremely loyal clientele. It started to bother Billy that I was making so much money. But he enjoyed the benefits the money brought with it. Billy couldn't make the kind of money I was making, so he saw my financial success as an opportunity to take some time off and focus on his music career. He played guitar beautifully and wrote gorgeous songs, and since Billy was talented and I loved him, I supported his dream of being a musician. I took out a loan and bought him thousands of dollars in music equipment, including a Les Paul guitar. I thought that, once he got on his feet in his career, he would be able to support my career goals. We had our dreams together and had it all mapped out, just as any young couple would.

My work schedule was grueling, but I believed I was working hard for both of us. Unfortunately, as time went on, Billy started focusing less on his music and more on partying.

Despite the long hours and the fast pace, or maybe because of it, I was living my life at work, involved with everyone, and then when I came home, it was just Billy and me and I'd be restless. It was difficult switching gears. I started going out with my friends to after-hours places that only people in the bar business went to. Billy would either come or not, depending on his mood, and then he stopped joining me and the others altogether. This was a new experience for me, going out without my fiancé by my side. People tended to see us as a married couple already. Then I started accepting people's invitations to dance, and I would intentionally dance closely with guys in the hopes that Billy would hear about it and get jealous. Of course our relationship began to deteriorate. Billy and I began to fight, whereas prior to this we'd never even had an argument or disagreement. Our relationship became more about making excuses not to see each other than trying to be together.

One night, I finished the second of my two waitressing jobs for the day, serving cocktails at Pier 66. I was waiting for Billy to pick me up by the entrance to the club when I encountered a bartender, Mark. It was getting late, and Mark was a bit surprised that I was still there. "Billy still isn't here? I could have sworn that I saw him pull up in your car about an hour ago."

"Really?" I replied. "Are you sure?"

I walked outside to the parking lot, and in the distance I saw my car and Billy leaning up against it. He wasn't alone. He was with another girl and they were making out, hot and heavy. He even had his hand up her shirt. As I walked closer, I realized that he was not only cheating on me with another girl, but that the girl was my close friend Debra.

I was wild with rage. Mark, sensing what was about to happen, ran up behind me, grabbed me by my waist, and held me back. He realized in a split second that something bad was going to happen. But even though Mark was a lot bigger than I was, he was no match for the strength that came over me. I don't know if it came from my anger or what, but I became a wiry little shit, kicking Mark hard and finally breaking free.

Well, I punched Debra so hard in the face that I knocked several of her teeth right out. That was the first time I ever punched anybody in my life. The only explanation I can come up with for that amount of strength is that as soon as I saw Debra with Billy, Nicky was present. I wasn't there anymore. Deciding to fight was *all* Nicky. Could I have handled it differently that night? Sure. It would probably have been better to walk away with dignity and grace, but I was so angry at this double display of disloyalty. In my book, Debra had done the worst thing you could ever do to another woman. Billy was *my* man. He was *my* property. I had kept Nicky tucked away for a while because I had Billy, but when Debra took Billy, I let Nicky come out and deal with her full force.

This was the man with whom I had my whole life planned. I was engaged to him. I believed in him. I believed in us. Whatever he needed—food, clothes, music equipment, whatever—I would have provided for him. I trusted him completely and he paid me back by going behind my back and hooking up with my friend.

Still furious, I hopped in my car and peeled out of the parking lot. My disappointment in the one person whom I'd trusted with my entire life was indescribable; I believe it was the first time in my life that I felt genuine heartache. I was stunned, hurt, and dazed beyond belief. All trust had been broken. Sure, we had a rocky relationship at the time, but I truly thought Billy and I were forever. He was not only my fiancé and lover but my best friend.

I immediately drove to the beach to try to clear my head and get a grip on my emotions. It dawned on me that Debra's husband was taking classes at a local college, and when I knew he would be at school, I took action—I drove to the campus and marched right into his classroom. As soon as he saw me, he knew I was crazy upset. Let's face it: I had good reason. I had been best of friends with his wife. When she had been drunk and throwing up, I held her head over the toilet and drove her home afterward. I gave her a couch to sleep on when she had a fight with her husband, and I helped them make up when they wanted to get back together. I was totally there for her. Seeing her with Billy was one of the most shocking and upsetting moments of my life thus far. Not surprisingly, I think that moment was when I began to not trust women.

Her husband hurried out of the classroom with a worried look on his face. I told him exactly what had happened.

"Your wife doesn't deserve your loyalty or my friendship! She knows all there is to know about Billy because we shared everything. I had no idea that she would take advantage of me and hook up with him!" I could barely catch my breath as the words came tumbling out. Eventually, I finished saying my piece and left him to his own thoughts.

After that, I kicked Billy out of the house. I was done with him, but he tried for some time to get back together with me. He would serenade me outside my home and follow me to bars and clubs, but I would more or less ignore him. He'd broken our trust and it was impossible for me to get it back. He should never have cheated on me. I couldn't ever respect or trust him after that. He blew it.

I would go out on dates, and no matter where I was or whom I was with, Billy would eventually show up. Since I'd know he was there, I would dance closely to whomever I was with on purpose, or I would sit with a group of guys and focus all my attention on the one speaking to me. I would hang on his every word so Billy could see what he was missing and how I'd moved on. It drove him crazy and I loved it because it was his turn to feel the way he had made me feel. It was his turn to hurt.

I began to hang out with people Billy couldn't keep up with—men who had more wealth and power than he could ever imagine existed. I was a newly single woman in Florida, and I was off to the races with a fast crowd.

5

LATINA NITEﾉ

n 1985 the nightlife in Miami was hotter than the weather. I was living at a pace that was catapulting me up the social ranks. When I wasn't working as a cocktail waitress, I'd spend my nights going to exclusive parties. I became a permanent fixture on the Miami club scene. I never had to wait in line to get into a club—ropes were parted for me and I was rushed inside like a celebrity straight to the VIP room.

Once I was in, I found it was easy to meet people, especially celebrities. Having a relationship during that time in Miami—whether the person was a celebrity or not—wasn't an easy go. If I simply hung out with a straight guy, we would be accused of messing around. (It was typically believed that you couldn't have a platonic relationship with someone of the opposite sex unless you or the other person was gay. I think that's complete bullshit. It may only rarely happen, but it *does* happen. I am living proof of it. I had and still have straight male friends who are really *just friends*—people I spend time with and have no romantic interest in.) In addition, after things ended with Billy, I didn't even know how I was going to *like* men again, let alone trust them.

I had to start all over again.

Part of my way of starting over was meeting an acclaimed Olympian, which happened while I was working as a cocktail waitress at September's. This Olympic legend came into the place quite often, and I served him, his publicist, and the rest of his entourage.

After a few of the athlete's visits, a friend of his phoned the owners of September's because he was trying to get in touch with me. The manager was completely blown away that this guy was calling and asking about me and not one of the other waitresses. Other pretty girls who worked at September's were considered the "it" girls—the waitresses whom everybody wanted to date and customers always inquired about. These typical Florida girls had perky, little, fit bodies, bright blue eyes, and long blond hair. There I was, looking quite the contrary, with curly brown hair, brown eyes, and a lean body. Unlike the rest of them, I wasn't dripping in jewel-studded gifts from rich South Florida men.

At first, the most exciting part was having people at work ask me about this Olympic athlete. *What was he like? Where did he take you?* I wasn't used to having people ask me anything about my private life or the guys I was seeing, so it was neat to have people suddenly care. I admit that the attention fed my ego. During my years with Billy, my life was more or less boring outside of work. I had small-town notions of settling down, and my friends were the people who knew me through Billy. In hindsight, I think they were moving a bit too slowly for me. All of a sudden I was in a much faster crowd and desired by men—powerful men.

I ended up dating the Olympic athlete and we had some fun together. He was kind of a rebound guy who I think I was into mainly because it would upset Billy. After a few dates we did have sex, but the relationship didn't have a big impact on me. He was a nice guy and a gentleman, but I wasn't in love with him, so I decided not to see him again. That was that.

My relationship with the star athlete helped me realize that I couldn't have sex with another man unless I was in love with him. I thought it was going to be easy to date again, but it proved to be much more difficult. I couldn't just be with someone for the heck of it. I had been with Billy for such a long time that I didn't know how to connect with a new guy physically. I was always expecting it to feel like love—the way Billy and I had felt when we made love. But when you're not in love with somebody, I discovered, it couldn't possibly feel like love. I was confused and had to discover all over again what love was going to be like.

Most of my partners were in a hurry to jump into bed with

me. However, I wasn't in much of a hurry to get into bed with just any man. I didn't have any particular complaints about sex, but I didn't enjoy superficial sex. I have never had a one-night stand in my life. Instead, I enjoyed having a relationship with a man. I liked knowing that he was going to be only with me. I also liked thinking that he was the only one I was going to be with as well. I had a deep desire to build trust with someone and to feel that we were working toward something of substance together.

It seemed like a waste to just give my body and soul to a man who wasn't going to say "Good morning" and "Good night" to me *every* single day and night. It's not that I had such an inflated sense of myself, it's just that in my subconscious I knew that I had to have respect for myself and my body after all that had happened during my childhood. My virginity had been taken from me without my permission so many years earlier, and in young adulthood I realized that I now had a choice— I could choose to have sex or not have sex with a man.

Kissing now became an integral part of my love life. In fact, kissing became more important to me than having sex. Sex was taken from me against my will, but nobody ever took a kiss from me. It was the only form of *my* sexuality that I actually had control over. If kissing is done passionately, properly, and with the right person, it feels better than sex. This has been proven to be true for me. I didn't take off my clothes, yet I got the same satisfaction and fulfillment. For a man, kissing probably isn't enough sexual pleasure, but for me, it was all I needed.

I never felt dirty from it. I didn't feel invaded or ever have to say to myself afterward, *What did I just do?*

Soon after my fling with the Olympian, a world-famous television star stumbled right into my new fascination with the art of kissing. It happened one night when I went with my girlfriends to the Grand in Coconut Grove. The Grand was a popular and trendy hotel with many bars, a hangout for the who's who of Miami at that time. That evening, I stepped into the elevator at the Grand to find Don Johnson standing right in front of me. He was really handsome—even better looking than he appeared on television—and Philip Michael Thomas, his costar on *Miami Vice,* was standing right next to him. In those days, these two guys were household names and on the covers of every top-selling entertainment magazine, and *Miami Vice* was one of the top-rated television shows in the country. Crockett and Tubbs with their white suits and pastel T-shirts underneath were a sensation. Men wanted to be them and women wanted to be with them. The hit cop show was shot on location right in Miami, so the cast were out and about at all the local hot spots almost every single night.

Don opened the conversation in a flirtatious way by telling me that I smelled really good and asking what I was wearing. I responded, "It's an oil, and I love it." (I still love it. Whenever I am around somebody who doesn't smell good to me, I put my wrist up to my nose and breathe in the oil to escape it. I do that to this day.)

Don and I continued our conversation about aromas. He

then asked me what I thought of the way he smelled. I said, "Let me have your wrist."

"No, it's on my neck," he said.

I smelled his neck and thought it smelled *very* good.

When you get close to someone's neck, you begin to feel each other's energy a bit. With our senses already heightened, a level of intrigue was definitely evolving between us. Whether the aroma banter was idle conversation or not, it didn't really matter. The scene in the elevator was getting sexier by the second.

Suddenly we were alone together in the elevator. Neither of us had realized our friends had already gotten out. Don gently placed his hand on the back of my neck, brushing my hair off to one side while pulling me toward him. He softly pressed his lips against my neck, near my ear. As he breathed on my neck, I began to feel aroused.

Don pulled me up against his body and we started kissing slowly. It wasn't one of those hard-core, faces-slamming-into-each-other make-out sessions, but passionate and sensual, and we ended up kissing for what felt like ages. We even stopped the elevator to continue and not be interrupted (the Grand had many elevators, so this wasn't a big deal). Don and I were kissing like two kids who were forbidden to see each other. When we finished, we checked our appearances in the mirror in the elevator, finally formally introduced ourselves, and politely shook hands. We started the elevator back up, and I pressed the floor where I was going. He said he was going to the same place ... the penthouse.

We were both headed to the same party. Once inside, Don and I separated, but we had our own little secret. For the rest of the night, we just shot each other knowing glances and smiles and got on with our evenings.

Don was a good kisser, and making out with him that night was like having sex for me.

On another occasion, I was at a modeling party and encountered the music legend Prince. All I am going to say is that he was the best kisser out of all the celebrities I have ever been with.

I realized over the years that being with a celebrity isn't more important than being with an average guy who appeals to you. Celebrity has never been a big deal to me. I wasn't impressed with stars' status or who they were professionally. They were just men in my eyes. I am more concerned about being with a man who truly loves me—at the end of the day, that's the only thing that counts, the basis for what can last forever.

———————

I stayed quite busy modeling and was making a good living for a young woman in her twenties. However, my girlfriend Tanya, who was modeling bathing suits just as often as I was, seemed to have a lot more money to spend. European designer shoes. Expensive designer clothing. Sports car. Dripping in jewelry. *What is she doing differently than me?* I thought.

One day, Tanya opened up and told me that she was getting paid through an agency to go on dates with men—wealthy businessmen—who would come to the South Miami area often. These successful moguls had their own planes, yachts, and endless amounts of cash to spend to have a good time, but due to their busy schedules, they had no time to look for women. They weren't interested in going out to dinner alone, traveling alone, yachting alone, etc. So Tanya was an available girlfriend whenever they arrived in town.

Tanya told me that she was a "regular" for three or four male clients. From working in the restaurant and bar business, I understood what a regular was. To me, that was someone who came into the same place on a regular basis, sat in my station, and tipped me well. Tanya informed me that her male clients didn't date other girls when they were in town, only her. I quickly became intrigued.

"Where do you go on dates with these men?" I asked.

"We only go to the finest restaurants and the hottest clubs," Tanya responded.

"Do you have to have sex with them?"

"It's not required and completely up to you."

"Is it safe to go out with these men?"

"Absolutely."

"How much do you make?"

"A thousand dollars an hour with a minimum of ten hours."

Wow, that's a lot of money, I thought. And in the 1980s, that was definitely a ton of money. I asked Tanya, "Do you think I have what it takes?" Tanya nodded yes and soon after introduced me to the head of the agency she worked for, which was technically termed a "call service."

Sharon was the boss—a robust forty-something woman who ran a tight ship. She was very intelligent and seemingly just as business-savvy as her mogul clients. However, underneath the tough exterior, I could tell there was a sweetness about her that put me at ease right away. In fact, the girls referred to Sharon as Mom because she kept everyone safe and treated us all equally.

Every client had to be checked out and verified first. Sharon hired a private detective who did background checks on all the people who wanted to use the call service. Also, if any potential client called asking about sex, the next thing they heard was a dial tone. Once checked out and accepted, the process was pretty straightforward. A client would describe preferences in body types, hair and eye color, height, ethnicity, age, etc. When Sharon found out what the customer desired, a date was set up and the client paid in advance.

The first date had some simple procedures for protection. For openers, the client was required to show his proper ID with photo. There was also a bodyguard who took us to meet the date and then stayed around to make sure we were safe. We had to update Sharon as to where we were at all times. The cell phones back in the eighties were the size of briefcases, so this wasn't a simple task. Instead, everyone carried a pager.

Sharon gave me some tips before she sent me out into the field. She explained, "Now you're a part of the family, and I just want you to know that whatever you decide to do behind closed doors is up to you. We can't protect you once you go into a home or hotel room. Sex is not a requirement. But if you do decide to have relations with somebody, I advise you to always practice safe sex. Other than that, just have a good time. Keep it safe. Keep it clean. And *always* keep us posted as to where you are."

I don't know what all of the girls who were in Sharon's employ did, but my girlfriend and I were paid by the hour. Am I sure that all of the girls at the agency were making the same money Tanya and I made per hour? I am quite certain they were not. However, we didn't exactly get together and talk about it. We were in direct competition with one another. I had no interest in what the rest of them were doing. I was more concerned with what I was doing, which was learning the business.

Prior to my first date, Tanya and I sat down, opened up a bottle of chardonnay, and had a heart-to-heart about the dos and don'ts of the business. One of the main rules was to develop a relationship with the client without quickly having sex with him. "Keep your hands to yourself and keep your eye on the prize," said Tanya, with the prize being a second, third, fourth date, etc. Next, she told me to never be distracted from my date no matter how gorgeous an onlooker might be. Furthermore, it's important to be overly impressed with what the client had to say without coming off as fake. "Less is best when it comes to speaking about yourself," Tanya said. "Nothing personal, but they don't really want to get to know you." I learned that in essence we were therapists for these men because they just really needed someone to talk to and share their time with.

Tanya asked me what my ideal date would be. My description included five-star dining and dancing, along with the finest wine and champagne money can buy. I'd also like to travel by limousine because it would be easier to have a conversation with my date and maintain eye contact. "But what does that have to do with what a man wants from me?" I asked her. Tanya told me that it had everything to do with it, because Sharon would set me up with the caliber of man who wanted that as well.

For my first date, I was picked up in a Rolls-Royce limousine. The man was named David and he was very good-looking, in his forties with dark hair and light eyes, and tall in stature. *He must have women throwing themselves at him,* I thought. *So that's exactly what I am not going to do.*

After our mutual introductions, curiously I asked him, "Where are we going?"

"To the airport," he responded.

"But this isn't the way to the airport."

"It is to the private airport where my personal jet awaits."

Pretty soon we were buckling up for takeoff, and I could see that he had done his homework when the stewardess brought over a bottle of my favorite champagne, Cristal Rose. While I listened to this handsome man talking, I sipped the Cristal, looked out the window, and thought, *I could get used to this.* I began to apply all of the advice that Sharon and Tanya spoke to me about. I remained focused and kept my "eye on the prize."

When we were landing, I could see snowcapped mountains, and it was clear that we weren't in Florida anymore. He told me to go to the back of the cabin, where the stewardess opened a closet filled with ski clothes for me. All of the clothes were the right size, too. He looked at me in the different outfits and chose what he wanted me to wear. When I exited the plane, I took on a whole new role—the role of David's girlfriend.

We spent the next three days together and David became my first regular. Soon after, a date with another man was arranged through the agency. Then, another and another. I ended up having four regulars who treated me very well. One was in his twenties, one in his thirties, and the other two were close to fifty. There was skiing in Aspen. Scuba diving in Saint Barts. Yachting down the Intercoastal in Florida. Over the next months, I embarked on some of the most exciting dates of my life.

Not every one was a fantasy date, though. There was one in particular where I arrived and I checked my date's ID and was surprised to find that his name did not match the one that was given to the agency prior. I immediately handed back his ID, excused myself, and departed. As I walked away, he said that he had never used this service before and felt they might lie to him about my description. He explained that he had used his friend's ID and everything was okay. That sounded all well and good, but I left anyway. On another date, the man checked out, but I had no connection with him whatsoever. He was wealthy but old, unattractive, and boring. No money in the world was worth me wasting my time like that.

It was clear that the men who used the agency wanted a woman who wasn't going to play all the games young girls do. They didn't want a clingy, needy, obsessive woman who wouldn't want to let them go once their travel time was up. The men's philosophy was basic: if you're playing games, you're not having fun. Two out of four of my men said their only goal was to have company and show me off in public on their arm. I was young and vivacious and wasn't hurting anyone. So I didn't mind being classified as "arm candy" one bit. They admired and never disrespected me. The other two were as gracious as the older gentlemen, but I personally felt them more as real relationships at that time.

The men and I never discussed any other relationships we might have been having. Part of the mystique is the unspoken rule not to discuss your private life or you would have just killed the mystery. For all they knew, I could have been in a very serious relationship. Maybe some of them had girlfriends.

However, nobody I dated on a regular basis ever wore a wedding ring. I find it hard to believe that any of these men were married because we spent the majority of our time together in public and frequented popular places in their hometowns. These men sometimes even introduced me to their friends and colleagues as their girlfriend.

Being a call girl meshed well with my personality. I despise wasting time. I didn't much care for commitment. And I was a free spirit. This to me was the perfect opportunity to expand on my theory, which was, why should I go out on a date just to go on a date and have it end poorly? And when the man doesn't get what he wants, which is sex, then you end up wasting your day getting ready or taking the night off from your various bartending jobs or missing time away from your friends. Nobody wants to wake up the next morning and complain about the night before. On the other hand, when I went on a date through the call service, it went exactly as I wanted it to. I knew what to expect and I had control over how it would end. I was sent limousines, flowers, outfits, and shoes, and I got paid for my time on top of it.

What I was doing was not illegal. On the other hand, soliciting sex *is*—better known as prostitution. And no one ever called me a prostitute until most recently, but I am not and I wasn't! I will no longer allow people's ignorance to continue, and that is why I am clearing this up. I was not paid to go up to men's hotel rooms. I was paid to establish relationships. I never got into trouble for being a girlfriend to anyone who needed a companion to go out with them in public. I can only imagine how scary it could be to be called to somebody's hotel room, and I am not judging those who have done it. But I don't know about that kind of situation because I was never involved in one.

Tanya told me that once I decided to be intimate with a client, I should understand that this is something the client would always expect from that moment on. I needed to make sure that before I opened the door to that possibility, the person was someone I wanted to be with. I took her advice into consideration before I ended up having physical relationships with the two younger men. It's simply that I was attracted to them and they were attracted to me, which seemed pretty normal as far as relationships go. In fact, once we got to that stage, we were already in the phase of our relationships where most people would be intimate with each other anyway. One of the two men genuinely developed feelings for me and asked me to be exclusive. However, I wasn't on the same page as him, and I was worried about my own feelings getting involved. I had already been deeply hurt by Billy, and that's when things began to get complicated. And it was at this point that this relationship as well as my career as a call girl would come to an end.

I spent six months working for Sharon and made a lot of money and developed some really great connections. I learned a lot about business from many of these successful men. I wasn't ashamed of working as a call girl then, and I am not ashamed that I ever did it. I think it's really different from what people generally imagine it to be. My job was to keep men company by going out with them. I was dropped off by security, treated very well, and picked up by security. I got to travel first-class and I was treated to expensive meals and champagne and shopping. Some might call this the best date they have ever had.

————

A turning point in my life occurred when I was twenty-four. I met a man named Jorge, who was more than twenty years older than me and was involved in and high up in a dark world, which at the time I knew nothing about.

When we first met at September's in the champagne room, what initially attracted me to this older South American gentleman was that he smelled incredible. His scent was trumped only by the way he behaved—he was a complete gentleman. When I poured him some wine, he would touch my hand to indicate his glass was full enough instead of telling me to stop. The way he touched my hand was more intoxicating than the wine: a lot can be communicated by such a simple act.

Our attraction was mutual right from the start. Jorge had something that I immediately wanted more of. From his scent to his manners to his intelligence, something was clearly special about him. He was deep and thoughtful and not loud at all. He never raised his voice once when speaking to me. (I am not saying that he never raised his voice to others, but I was never around when he did.) He was confident and in control of his environment at all times, and I found this alluring.

Women were always throwing themselves at Jorge, and those very women were the ones he couldn't seem to stand. He never even made eye contact with women who attempted to flirt with him and get his attention. Instead, he would look directly into my eyes. Jorge didn't like to see women acting as if they were easy or sleazy. He liked a woman to act like a lady. I think he liked a woman he could teach as well, and I think he saw that in me.

From the moment Jorge and I met, we were inseparable. In a nonpossessive way he wanted to make sure I was okay every waking moment of the day. Jorge took me out to many fabulous restaurants in the Miami area, and after dinner we went out dancing at popular Latino clubs. He used to love to watch me dance. However, when I was with him, men were not allowed to touch me when I went out onto the dance floor. Jorge made sure of that. Other people would stand around me and he would watch as I danced safely. I enjoyed dancing in a safe little bubble. It made me feel secure and important, like a princess. That was what Jorge called me: his princess. He certainly treated me like one. He never disrespected me and never made me cry or feel belittled or stupid because I didn't know something. He took an interest in what I enjoyed doing and quickly learned that one of my passions was horseback riding. Jorge would often take me riding, even though he didn't ride himself; he made a lot of effort to ensure my happiness.

Jorge was a businessman, who would only occasionally crack a smile. Because he had a dimple on one side of his face, his smile was kind of crooked, which I thought was cute and endearing. He didn't show that smile to anyone other than me, and it made me feel that I was really adored by him. I know he really loved me as I did him.

I kept working at September's for a while longer after meeting Jorge, but shortly thereafter there was no need to continue. Jorge was not comfortable with my working there and he was happy to support me. He wanted me all to himself and felt that he could concentrate better on his business that way. I was present for some of his business meetings—often the only woman at the table—but I never asked questions (besides, his associates usually didn't speak English; they spoke Spanish, which I don't understand all that well). Despite the language barrier, I learned a lot of life lessons from being there. I am smart enough always to keep my mouth shut, especially when I'm under verbal attack. Being around Jorge taught me that.

When people say, "Do you know who I know?" I laugh to myself and think, *No, I don't. I don't even think you know who you know!* Nobody I was ever around who was part of Jorge's world *ever* talked about whom they knew. Nobody whom I have been around in the past forty-seven years of my life who was *really* connected *ever* had to brag about whom they knew. It was just understood. In that world, you don't have to name-drop. These guys don't threaten people. There is no reason to—they are all doers, not talkers.

It didn't matter to me what business Jorge was in, I just loved him and felt safe when I was with him. He could have been selling vacuums for all I cared. Our relationship did not merely consist of partying and doing superficial things together; we had a relationship of substance. Jorge and I had a baby together, but unfortunately the baby did not survive. As anyone would agree, it is difficult to lose a child. I think it was especially difficult for me because I was adopted; it would have been my first chance at a real family. But it wasn't meant to be. It was another one of those lessons that I had to learn the hard and painful way. Now I understand that this was a part of my journey, and today I am so grateful for my two beautiful daughters and I know my son will always be watching from above.

Another great lesson Jorge taught me was to observe what is going on around me at all times and have presence of mind—*always*. The day I was arrested, I was clearly not paying attention to the vital life lessons that Jorge had taught me.

On June 23, 1986, I returned from modeling at a photo shoot hopeful to see my boyfriend, but to no avail. When I walked into the place where I was eventually arrested, to my surprise I saw one of my neighbors, who appeared to be beaten up and high on cocaine.

One night at a club a few months prior, I had introduced my neighbor to a few acquaintances of mine. In the hot Miami nights, everybody is friends with everybody, so I introduced them as my friends. It wasn't meant to be an introduction for business purposes, but it unfortunately ended up that way, and now I was caught right in the middle. My neighbor was obviously involved in a drug deal gone bad, and to assess the damage, I tried to get some answers out of him.

"What are you doing here?" I asked.

"They stole the shit, man. The Jamaicans stole it, all of it!" he said.

"What shit? What Jamaicans? And what are you talking about?"

"The coke."

"What?! Please tell me you paid these people. If they don't get their money, they are not going to be happy."

"That's why I'm here."

"That's why you got the shit kicked out of you, too. This is not good. I introduced you to them and now it looks like you've robbed them. Are you a fucking idiot? Don't tell me you robbed these people."

He didn't answer.

I tried to quickly piece the story together. From what I gathered, my neighbor had been given drugs to deliver. He was to collect $24,000 for the goods and bring the money back to the supplier. However, he claimed to have been robbed by some Jamaicans along the way. The whole story didn't add up. I wasn't buying it and, more important, neither was anyone else. The bottom line is that, with these people, you don't take what isn't yours.

My neighbor appeared to have been roughed up. However, he didn't seem to have been kidnapped. He wasn't tied up or restrained in any way; on the contrary, he was sitting comfortably in an easy chair snorting coke. I determined from the fast-food wrappers strewn all over the place that he wasn't being starved, either. It didn't appear that anybody was keeping him there against his will. I assumed he didn't ask if he could leave because that would be sure to piss off his new enemies.

I knew that the reason he probably was able to walk out with the drugs in the first place without paying for them was because he had claimed to be an acquaintance of mine. He had clearly used me and used my name. Yes, I had introduced him to those guys, but what they did from that point on should have been none of my business. However, because he had screwed them over, it *became* my business.

My neighbor tried to dupe them and made me look really bad. If I left, the guys he'd stolen from would probably have thought that I was involved. The more I think about it over the years, the more I believe that he was hoping they would blame me and hurt me for his misdeeds. What a coward! But what he didn't count on was that I had already built trust with them, so while I had introduced them to a bad business partner, I wasn't going to take the fall for his stupid actions.

After I'd pieced together the info I got out of him, his father called. I had a brief conversation with him about the $24,000 debt that his son owed and that needed to be paid in full immediately. I believe that phone conversation was taped by the authorities, making me an accessory.

Moments later, I heard some loud sounds of complete chaos outside the house. Voices over megaphones began shouting orders: "Come out with your hands up!"

I immediately began to panic. I had no idea who was issuing the orders or why. I didn't even know if they were talking to me. The house phone rang and I answered reluctantly. A voice on the other end of the line told me to come outside.

I could feel every fiber of my being tremble as my heart beat out of my chest. I could hear it pounding in my ears.

"Just come out of the house and everything will be okay," said a man who turned out to be a federal agent.

I eventually came out of the house, still shocked and totally unaware of what was happening. However, I was positive that it was not a good situation and I had no idea how to handle it. After all, I thought things like this only existed in the movies.

I went out the front door, and unlike what I had seen in the movies, the feds didn't tackle me to the ground. Instead, they matter-of-factly asked me to put my hands where they could see them. In my fear and confusion I did just that, and everything else they asked me to do, while shaking uncontrollably. The federal agents asked if any weapons were in the house, and I answered, "No, not that I'm aware of." They asked if I had any weapons on me, despite the fact that I was wearing shorts and a T-shirt and clearly couldn't have concealed anything bigger than a toothpick. However, I didn't want to point out the obvious (I wanted the authorities to see the little girl in me who was genuinely afraid), so I simply said no. They searched me and quickly found out that I was telling the truth. Then they read me my rights and handcuffed me, and I was put in the back of a police car.

As I sat in the back of the car with one of the FBI agents, a SWAT team and various federal agents systematically went in and out of the house, carrying boxes of stuff, and I saw a lot of smoke drifting out of the house. I didn't know what they were doing or what any of it meant. As I watched, several questions ran through my mind: *What are they going to ask me? What is this about? How am I going to answer their questions?* I wished there were someone I could call and ask what the hell I was supposed to do. However, I wasn't so confused that I didn't know something major was going on, although I suspected what it might be about. One thing was for sure: I didn't know the true gravity of the situation, which would unfold in the days to come.

Time seemed to be standing still, and the events taking place appeared to be happening in slow motion. I felt as if I were in a bad dream. Unfortunately, it wasn't a dream at all.

I was finally taken down to the local FBI headquarters, where they interrogated me for the better part of three days. I was put into a cell for the nights and removed in the mornings for more shitty food and endless questioning.

Eventually I was transported to a Florida penitentiary where I would await my arraignment. I made the three-hour trip accompanied by FBI agents in their car. They told me that I was being driven by them, instead of my going on the prison bus, because it was safer for me since I was a high-profile arrest. I never fully understood what they meant by that.

Going through the prison gates and seeing the buses pull up filled with prisoners was a wake-up call that I will always remember. Once I was inside, they made me strip naked for a body search, and they were not delicate about it. As I walked handcuffed through the prison, I saw myself on the news on a television. It was a shattering sight.

I was put into cell block C. Thirty cells were in the block, with two women in each cell. Many of the women were gang members. I could immediately tell I didn't belong there—inmates were there doing major time for serious crimes. We were in a state penitentiary, and the feeling was in the air that nobody was going anywhere, ever. I was slated to be there for three weeks pending an arraignment in front of a judge.

At lockdown, I went into my assigned cell inside the block, which was pretty scary. I didn't have to share a cell with anyone; apparently that was to protect me. The cell was tiny—it fit two bunks and a toilet that was close to the ground. That was it. I suffered from claustrophobia, but I had to get over that real quick.

The first nights I spent in prison I didn't get a lot of sleep. I lay in my bed and began to think that if I continued living the destructive lifestyle I was living, I would die young. I started to actually appreciate getting arrested. Once and for all, I had to make changes in my life, and this was the swift kick in the ass I needed to do so. I also realized that there must be something important that I was supposed to live for, a bigger purpose. I began thinking about having children, and as I lay on my prison bunk, I wondered what my kids would look like. I thought about what had happened between Billy and me. I got really sad thinking about my horrible family life and all my brothers who had died. Being in prison gave me time to reflect on everything and everybody that had had an impact on my life.

The day after I arrived at the penitentiary, Norman Elliott Kent, my attorney, came to see me. Jorge had arranged for him to represent me. Norman wore crisp tailored suits and was incredibly focused. He was a big-shot attorney in Dade County whose forte was bad boys, and I was certainly a bad boy—or rather, a bad girl. I had no clue how the system worked or how this process was going to go. This bad girl was crying and scared. Norman calmed me down and began to advise me both legally and personally.

During our first meeting Norman advised me not to show my emotions. It was a sign of weakness to the other prisoners. He told me that they prey upon weakness in these places and I already stood out enough as it was. Then he advised me not to take a shower—it was too dangerous. He said everyone would see me naked and I could get raped. *I can't take a shower for three weeks? Okay, wonderful,* I thought. Luckily, later that day, my girlfriend Alex brought me deodorant, a toothbrush, toothpaste, and commissary money. She also brought me my favorite red velvet Fila sweat suit, which was popular and fashionable at that time in Miami. I remember feeling particularly grateful that she'd brought that warm-up suit because wearing it made me feel safe and gave me a sense of home.

———

A few days later I was sitting at a table near a group of other inmates who began to pick on me. They were starting to mark their territory, and one of the girls wanted me to be her "bitch." Clearly, this situation was going to turn really bad, really fast.

As I was starting to panic, a black woman named Sister Sue came along. She resided in the first cell of the block, near the pay phone. Now, let me explain the importance of this in prison life. When you live inside a cell block and the phone is right outside your cell, that sends a message. You don't get to pick your cell as if prison were a summer camp. There's no "Oh, I want that bunk!" Her cell location was a clear sign that Sister Sue had a lot of respect and authority within cell block C.

Sister Sue's meth lab had exploded, and that was why she got arrested and ended up in prison. Sue looked as if she had been doing her fair share of meth. She had missing teeth and her skin was weathered and I believe she might have been in her thirties, but she looked much older.

Sister Sue approached the table and said to me in a cold, commanding voice, "You have a phone call."

"Oh, really? Okay," I answered sheepishly.

When I got to the pay phone to take the call, Sister Sue said quietly, "You're going to act like you're talking on the phone. Understand?"

"Okay."

"I told whoever was calling that you couldn't talk."

"Who called?"

"What am I, your secretary? Do you want to survive this place?"

"Yes."

She then brought me into her cell. "Get down on your knees and close your eyes," she demanded.

I did what I was told. Tears began rolling down my face and I was shaking like a leaf. I had no idea what was going to happen. Then I heard a thud. Something hard had hit the mattress. (There are no fluffy mattresses in prison, so it was a pretty loud noise.)

"Now open your eyes," Sister Sue said. I opened my eyes slowly and saw . . . a Bible.

"When you're done reading this psalm, I will protect you," she said. "I'm in here for a while and I'm not going anywhere. Sure, you might get out. But while you're here, I'll take care of you."

"Okay. Thank you," I said, relieved.

I stayed on my knees and read the Bible. When I was done, Sister Sue kept her word and gave me her protection. Nobody—and I mean nobody—messed with me again. Prior to that, I wasn't able to eat regularly and the other prisoners took everything I owned. Sister Sue got all my stuff back. When I took a shower, Sister Sue watched over me, but she never made advances toward me. Some of the other women inmates were hard-core gang members, but they didn't scare Sister Sue. Finally, somebody was watching my back in cell block C.

Shortly after I arrived in prison, Billy reached out to me. He had seen me on the news and decided to visit me. I didn't actually want to see him, but when I was told he was there, I felt guilty and decided to meet with him. He told me he still loved me and would always be there for me, and I told him that I was in a different place in my life and it was a frightening moment for me. Then I began to blame him for my ending up in prison. In retrospect, it wasn't my smartest move, but I wanted him to feel like shit for cheating on me.

"I wouldn't have been sent here if you didn't cheat on me," I said.

Billy told me that he felt horrible about it. *Ah, I hit a nerve,* I thought. Then I decided to embellish on my current situation to make him feel truly terrible: I told him that I had been extremely ill in sick bay and a guard had tried to rape me. Billy was upset and angered by the news. I saw the jealous reaction that I had longed for, and it was the perfect antidote to my misery.

Sadly, my lie almost ended up coming true. I got sick and asked to be taken to sick bay for medical attention. Male prison guards were taking care of female prisoners, and I was escorted by one of them from my cell. When this happens, the other prisoners lean out of their cells and watch you walk by them down the long, straight hallway. If you fall out of sight during the walk to sick bay, the prisoners know something's up, something's wrong. On my way to sick bay, the guard pushed me into a storage closet and out of sight. In a flash, he pulled my pants down. The guard stuffed a rag into my mouth and had me bare from the waist down and lying on my stomach with my hands cuffed behind my back.

Out of nowhere, Sister Sue came to my rescue. She burst into the closet and yelled, "Get off her, now!" He didn't. He had given her no choice, so Sister Sue shanked the guard in the leg. Like many of the other prisoners, Sister Sue had a makeshift knife made from whatever was available because everyone had to protect themselves come nightfall. The danger wasn't so much because of the other prisoners. The real danger was from the prison guards—something I'd just learned firsthand and wouldn't soon forget.

6

TRIAL AND RESOLUTION

As the date for my bail hearing drew near, I began thinking of what I was going to do when I got out of jail. Whom would I see first? What would I want to eat for my first meal? Then harsh reality set in: what if I was denied bail and sent right back to jail? This was becoming a real possibility as I spent weeks watching it happen to countless prisoners before me.

Certain days during the week at the Florida penitentiary were designated as either arraignment or trial days. Female prisoners would spend the early mornings putting on makeup, spraying on perfume, and getting dressed in their best outfits to hopefully make a good impression on the judge. Before the bus ride to court, they would be bound in shackles and put in handcuffs, then escorted outside.

Most prisoners were fearful, some even crying as they left, because they knew this might be their last chance at freedom for a long time. If the verdict went their way, they could walk out of the courtroom as free women and see their families again. If they didn't get released that afternoon, their next shot might be in another year, five years, ten years, maybe longer.

Sadly, at the end of the day I watched many of the women who'd got dressed up in the morning full of hope come back to jail, devastated because things hadn't gone their way. Even the most hardened criminals looked shattered when that happened. I remember looking around and thinking how awful it would be if I had to stay in there for God knew how much longer. I thought to myself that if I did have to stay, I should start becoming better friends with these women. But I didn't become closer with any of them because in my mind befriending them meant that I was going to have to stay in jail. A back-and-forth tennis match ensued in my head as the days went on. I became more scared and thought deeply while in my cell—a prisoner within my own thoughts.

Then I met Isabella, who helped me garner some inner strength.

When she arrived, Isabella immediately stood out from the rest of the prisoners. She walked into jail wearing Gucci sneakers and carrying Louis Vuitton luggage, a natural Spanish beauty with flawless skin and a body that was in phenomenal shape. She obviously took good care of herself.

Isabella and I hit it off right away. She told me that, along with her husband, she had been a successful drug dealer, and one of the keys to their success in the drug trade was that they were not users. (It's well-known that drug addicts don't make good dealers, since they end up blowing their own profits, so to speak. Like Isabella, many successful dealers handled drugs strictly as merchandise and applied the Tony Montana *Scarface* rule of "never get high on your own supply.")

Isabella was sentenced to a year-and-a-half prison term. However, she said she'd be up for an early release in nine months if everything went well. She and her husband had another business, totally legitimate, that they earned income from. The couple made enough money from that business so that they didn't even need to deal drugs. They did it because they desired to go from wealthy to *extremely* wealthy and felt that it was worth the risk to be able to afford a lifestyle they had always dreamed of. A yacht, a private plane, and expensive cars were all at their fingertips due to their ill-gotten gains. The most difficult part about doing hard time for Isabella was being away from her children, and if she could have done it over again, she would have given it all up to be able to tuck her kids into bed every night. When you're behind bars, you quickly realize what's most important in life. Yachts and cars don't mean a thing when you can't see your children. Thankfully, Isabella and her husband did not lose their home when they got arrested. The law at that time was that if you had a home and kids, you could keep the house as long as it wasn't purchased with money from the sale of illegal drugs. Luckily, Isabella was able to prove that her home had been legitimately financed. Although she missed her kids terribly, Isabella was pragmatic. She had been caught and accepted her fate. "Hey, I did the crime and now I have to do the time," she matter-of-factly said.

On the day of my bail hearing, I got dressed in an all-black suit outfit that my friend Alex had picked out for me at a department store and brought to the prison. I didn't have a lot of businesslike clothes at home in my closet—I spent my days in Miami running around in tiny bikinis and my nights at clubs in designer dresses.

Isabella stopped by my cell to offer me a few words of advice and encouragement before I headed to court, which I needed as I prepared to leave my cell and face the unknown.

"Whatever you imagine that you'll get is probably exactly what you'll get," she began calmly. "Remember, they are like hound dogs. If you go into court scared, they will instantly pick up the scent of fear. Being scared is a sign of weakness, and a sign of weakness is a sign of guilt. Everything flows as one." I nodded my head as she continued: "If you're strong, they'll also pick up on that. A sign of strength is a sign of confidence. And when you're confident, they'll feel you're not guilty. You need to visualize and internalize what you want. If you don't believe it yourself, it won't happen, so believe and don't be scared. Be strong."

Isabella and a few of the other girls walked me down to the exit of the cell block as I began my journey to court. When we reached the door, Isabella put her arms around me and said, "Have a good life." I knew exactly what she was trying to do. She was instilling the power of positive thinking in me. If I didn't think I would be coming back to prison, then I wouldn't be coming back. The first step was believing it myself.

I smiled. "Thanks, you have a good life, too."

The name Isabella, translated from Spanish into English, means "goddess of plenty." Isabella was exactly that.

I went to court with a positive attitude and it paid off. My bail was set at $10,000, which Jorge paid for me. I was a free woman, but for how long I didn't know. I also knew that with the investigation and pending trial I couldn't see Jorge again, and this was heartbreaking. It seemed that whenever I finally found love in my life, it was always taken from me. I wondered when this pattern would finally change.

When I left court, I was like a lost puppy, skittish and vulnerable. After almost a month in prison, all I wanted was to sleep in my own bed, but I couldn't go home right away. I was advised that until my case went to trial, it would be best if I stayed with a friend.

I ended up staying with Alex and her sister for a couple of weeks. Alex's brother-in-law and I would stop by my house occasionally to pick up my clothes and mail. They were like family and I felt safe and at home around them. Alex made comfort food and helped me readjust to normal life. After I got arrested, I learned who my friends were. Many of my old acquaintances avoided me, while a few others embraced me and supported me in ways I couldn't have imagined. I didn't realize it then, but this arrest would lead me to be scrutinized by others. People would judge me for decades to come because of this one arrest, and no matter what I did to make things right, this event would overshadow everything and would continually come back to haunt me. However, I've never been ashamed of it. I tell people honestly what happened to me. It was a part of my life and it's what I went through. I've met many hypocrites and fair-weather friends, but when I've opened up and told my real friends what happened, they haven't run. They say, "I don't really care about that incident. I care about *you*."

I had kept in touch with my mom while I was in Florida. After my arrest and while I was on bail, she was instrumental in gathering letters of reference from upstanding citizens who knew me throughout my childhood. Doctors, teachers, and lawyers wrote about how I was a good student, how I never got into trouble, etc. My mother wasn't focused on what I had done wrong, she was more concerned with my safety. I never had the kind of relationship with my mother or father where I would ask them their opinions or consult them on what I wanted to do in my life. However, if something serious happened, my mother would try her best to be there for me. This was one of those times, and I was extremely grateful for her support.

Over the weeks following my release on bail, I met often with my attorney. I was pleased to hear that drug cases were not foreign to him. Norman Elliott Kent had handled two high-profile marijuana cases, and he had been covered in the *New York Times* and was the focus of a lead story on NBC for suing the state of Florida for spraying paraquat, an herbicide that destroys the environment as well as plant life, on marijuana. In various agrarian areas of Florida, people were cultivating marijuana, and the federal government, under Ronald Reagan's direction, had launched a campaign to spray paraquat on the fields. My attorney reached an agreement with the U.S. government stating they were not to spray paraquat on marijuana. In another case, Norman represented a grandmother with glaucoma who was in trouble for cultivating marijuana for use to ease her condition. He won that case on the grounds that the pot was a medical necessity.

I had no clue how the legal system worked. Up until my arrest my only brush with the law had been receiving a speeding ticket. Norman explained in detail the road ahead. When the federal government wants to charge somebody with a crime, it can do it through one of two ways: first, they can opt to arrest you and file what is called an "information." Or, they can present the charges to a grand jury, which consists of twenty-three citizens who vote on the matter at hand. My case was to be presented to a grand jury. Unlike a regular jury in a case, the decision made by the grand jury does not have to be unanimous. It just has to be a majority.

When I stood before the grand jury in Florida, I had eight indictments against me. The grand jury charged everyone named in the case, and the government then figured out whom it wanted to make deals with. The prosecutors decided that they wanted to make a deal with me.

Although I was deathly afraid of going to prison, I wasn't sure that I wanted to make a deal, either. I knew that I was innocent of the eight counts against me, but my attorney kept telling me that going to trial was not a good idea. I was considered an accessory, and if I pleaded innocent, they could try me on each count separately. Every count would get its own trial, and I would have to prove my innocence on each one. If I was found guilty, each of the counts was punishable by up to nineteen years in prison.

Behind the scenes, my attorney conferred with one of the prosecutors, Theresa Van Vliet, and learned that they wanted me to plead guilty to kidnapping and extortion, the least of all the charges. For my cooperation, they would suggest to the judge that I receive probation. *Kidnapping? How could I kidnap a grown man? Extortion? Will that be on my permanent record?* I had so many questions, and I felt that everything I had been taught about telling the truth and everything that I believed in was not applicable here. The case was more about circumstances and timing—I just happened to be in the wrong place at the wrong time. My attorney kept trying to get it through my thick skull that regardless of whatever I had or hadn't done, I was there and being charged for the crimes. To the powers that be, I was guilty by association. Nobody wanted to know what I had or hadn't done. What they really wanted to know was what I was willing to take responsibility for. However, I kept saying I hadn't done anything, and that I was innocent.

My attorney assured me that it was virtually unheard-of to get probation based on charges as serious as the ones I was facing. Also, the deal I was offered couldn't have been worked out without the cooperation of prosecutor Van Vliet and the belief that she had in me. She clearly took a leap of faith on my credibility and ability to bounce back while facing extreme adversity, and I wasn't going to let her down. I wasn't going to let myself down, either.

I decided that my best option was to take the plea agreement.

While I was awaiting my court case, I hung out quite a bit with a friend of mine named John Uribe. He would stop by my house mostly late at night, and we would have many long talks until the sun came up. I first met Kevin Maher through John.

I didn't know this at the time, but while I was out on bail and my trial was pending, John began to get paranoid about my flipping on him. His mind raced with thoughts that I was going to do something underhanded, such as rat him out to the authorities. Doing something like that had never crossed my mind, but John wasn't thinking clearly. His paranoia was a result of his excessive use of cocaine. In an attempt to make himself feel more secure, John phoned Kevin in New Jersey and asked him to come down to Miami to check me out.

I wasn't aware of the intricacies of John and Kevin's business and personal relationship back then. I found out later that Kevin was using John to find criminals for the DEA to lock up. Kevin would make frequent trips down to Miami, then return with new information for his DEA contacts in New York City. I find it rather ironic that John called Kevin down to Miami to make sure I wasn't a rat, and in the end Kevin locked John up.

Kevin drove down to Miami in his Porsche, all the way from New Jersey, to the Mayfair nightclub, where I was hanging out in the VIP room. Contrary to previous reports, that evening I was *not* wearing leather hot pants with my leg over a chair with no underwear. I was actually dressed quite tastefully in a long, fitted, ruffled Spanish dress.

Kevin stuck out like a sore thumb as soon as he walked into the trendy Latin nightclub. While I fit in with my dark, tanned skin and long, curly hair, he was quite the opposite: a pale-skinned, Irish American guy with bright blue eyes.

Kevin saw me from across the room and approached me with a stoic seriousness. "Where's John?"

"Who are you?" I responded.

"I'm Kevin. Kevin Maher. I'm from New Jersey and John called me."

"Well, then you have his phone number," I answered bluntly.

"Don't be a smart-ass with me. I know who you are . . . Beverly."

"Oh, you're smart, too," I shot back, and began to turn away. "Everybody in here knows who I am. Did you ask the doorman my name? Anyway, I don't really want to talk to you."

Kevin walked away and came back up to me a bit later that night. That time, he was severely pissed off. John had gotten the keys to Kevin's Porsche from the valet and taken off with it. Even though Kevin had rubbed me the wrong way when I first met him, for some reason at that moment I felt bad for him. Since he appeared to be a cop, I knew that nobody at the club was going to help him get his car back, so I decided to lend a hand.

I told Kevin that I would go down to the valet with him and help look into the problem. He seemed to appreciate my offer, and when we got into the elevator to go down to the valet, he looked at me rather funny. Not ha-ha funny, but as if he were going to lean over and kiss me. I was dead right. We began kissing, and although it seemed strange, I went with it.

When we got to the lobby, I told Kevin not to tell John what had just happened between us. I wasn't involved with John romantically, but I didn't know exactly why Kevin was in

Miami, and somehow things didn't seem to add up. John and Kevin clearly didn't march to the same drummer, and I strongly suspected that there was more to their involvement than met the eye.

Once we got to the valet, Kevin called up John on his car phone and told him to return his car immediately. Kevin was screaming at John, but John didn't come back with the car. After a couple of hours went by, I began to feel even worse for Kevin.

As we waited for John to return from his joyride with Kevin's Porsche, hopefully in one piece, we opened up to each other. Finally, he hit me with it: "I'm with the FBI," Kevin said quietly. *I knew he was a cop*, I thought.

"Just stop!" I insisted. "I don't want to know anything about what you're doing. I have my own problems right now."

"Yeah, John told me you were arrested and that you're out on bail. He's paranoid that you're going to get him locked up."

"What?!" I was stunned. "I'm not trying to have John locked up. I'm done with my case. Finished. And I don't want to go back. Not ever."

Kevin said he could help me.

"How can you help me? I'm already done with my case." I told Kevin that in just a few weeks I was going to go before the judge to be sentenced. I had already pleaded guilty to extortion and was getting a plea bargain, which included probation.

"I'll *make sure* that you get probation," Kevin insisted.

"You don't have to make sure. I've already done it all through my attorney. Please don't interfere with this."

He looked me in the eye and said, "I just want to keep you safe."

When Kevin said that, I melted instantly. I hadn't heard a man offer to keep me safe in a long time. I was insecure, upset, anxious, and scared. For a brief moment after he offered me safety, the darkness then surrounding my life became a bit lighter. Kevin wasn't my type; I had previously dated tall, dark, and handsome Latino men, and he was short, pale, and not the best-looking guy. However, he said those magic words at a time in my life when they mattered. At that moment, our connection grew deeper, and for me this went far beyond the physical.

"I don't want your help right now," I responded softly. "But when I'm done with my case, it would be nice to know that somebody's there for me, because one thing's for sure—I have to get out of Miami when this is all over."

He took a deep breath and said, "I'm in love with you."

What? I wondered how this man could already be in love with me when we had just met. I didn't even know him, and he certainly didn't know me. But when you're young, in trouble, and fighting for your life, you don't question things that feel positive, and it felt good and reassuring to hear. I was to learn in time that Kevin's love wasn't really love at all—it was an obsession. My problem was that I didn't know it at that moment. How could I have known?

In November of 1986, I entered court to hear my sentence. My lawyer told me that while it looked good, courts don't have to accept plea agreements. They can reject them if they so choose. I held my breath and prayed. Prosecutor Van Vliet walked over to the defense side of the table and told Judge Eugene Spellman that she was going to recommend probation and gave all the reasons why. When she was finished, Judge Spellman asked me to stand up.

The judge lowered his glasses down on his nose and looked directly into my eyes. Before he sentenced me, he wanted to inform me that in the seventeen years he had sat on the bench, he had never had a prosecutor recommend probation for charges as serious as mine. Not ever. Judge Spellman let me know unequivocally that if I messed up and landed back in court, I should not look for help from Van Vliet, and he would specially request to be assigned my case and would put me away, personally.

Then Judge Spellman gave me my sentence: five years' probation.

Contrary to various reports, I never ratted anyone out. As part of my plea bargain, I was prepared to testify truthfully about the events that unfolded. However, the other people named in the case made plea bargains for themselves and never went to trial. My testimony was never required. I didn't rat my boyfriend out, either. Jorge paid for my defense, so when people accuse me of betraying him, it makes no sense whatsoever. If the arrest hadn't happened the way it happened and I had been involved with somebody else at the time, I really could have gone downhill. It was actually a gift that I had received my wake-up call when I did and had supportive people in my life, and I don't have any regrets.

My attorney, Norman Elliott Kent, recently reflected on my arrest, trial, and subsequent rehabilitation that brought me to the positive state of my present life:

Danielle met the demanding requirements for pretrial release, including significant drug rehabilitation counseling, which requires a lot of energy. She undertook the difficult task of accepting responsibility for her own actions, and she wanted to do whatever was necessary to remain a free woman and change her life. Danielle was rewarded for her efforts by the prosecutor when she was recommended for probation. None of these things that she is achieving now as a television star would be possible today had she not taken those ameliorative and rehabilitative measures back then. If Danielle did not take these kinds of brave steps, instead of starring on a television show, she might be just getting out of prison and in a halfway house. Only her willingness to change in the past made her future possible. If you want to be better tomorrow, the time to start is today.

One of the conditions for my probation was that it had to be served outside of Miami. The prosecutor and my attorney spoke at great length about how unsafe and unhealthy it would be for me to stay there any longer, and the judge agreed and wanted an address where I would be relocating within three days of my sentencing. I had no family or any real friends outside of Miami and had no idea where I was going to move, so my attorney requested an extension while I put the pieces of my potential new life together. I quickly began to drift back into my old bad habits, going out to clubs and partying all night. I wasn't drinking or doing drugs; instead, I was getting high on what I loved the most—dancing. I finally had my freedom back and wanted to celebrate on the dance floor. I also wanted to reclaim the carefree feeling that I had enjoyed in Miami before everything went sour.

My attorney caught wind that I was resorting to my old ways. Miami may seem large, but in my circles word traveled fast. One night, one of the club owners who was a friend of my attorney suggested that I should leave Miami because he'd hate to see me get into trouble again. It didn't take me more than a moment to realize that he was right.

It was hard leaving Miami behind, but it was time. So that's exactly what I did.

7

ONE STEP FORWARD, TEN STEPS BACK

t was time to take charge of my life, but my support system was weak. I had no contact with my father and barely spoke to my mother. I had no boyfriend, and all of my close friends were in Florida, a place where I could no longer stay. I had to leave everything I had known for the past seven years and start a new chapter of my life somewhere else. Probation was to last for the next five years; my goal was to complete my probation without incident and put this Miami phase of my life far behind me. It would be difficult, but I was up to the challenge when I considered the alternatives. At the time, moving to New Jersey with Kevin seemed to be a smart option. In fact, it was my only option.

Kevin constantly stayed in touch with me after we met at

the club. Let's put it this way: we were more than just friends. He was traveling back and forth to Florida and he made it a point to find me and see me when he was in town. He told me many more times that he loved me and promised over and over to keep me safe. After a stint in prison, having eight serious indictments against me, and receiving probation (by the skin of my teeth and the grace of God), that's exactly what I needed to hear. Plus, Kevin had told me he was an FBI agent—a man of the law. Starting the next phase of my life with someone who could truly protect me seemed like the perfect fit.

When I finally told Kevin that I wanted to leave Florida and be with him after months of his trying to convince me, he was quite happy, to say the least. We drove all the way to the Garden State in his Porsche, and as soon as we arrived, Kevin put me up in a motel in Little Ferry, which is a blue-collar town just south of Hackensack. It was the kind of motel where you pay by the hour, not by the night, and it was riddled with hookers, drugs, and pimps. Used needles and empty plastic baggies containing drug residue were actually in the corner of my room when I checked in. I couldn't bear to sleep in the bed—the pillows and bedspread were so full of stains that I wouldn't even venture to sit on it. I unpacked some of my clothes and draped them over a chair, the only reasonably clean piece of furniture in the room. That was where I would sit during the day and sleep at night. The bathroom was no better—it was disgusting. I would put on sweatpants and a baseball hat pulled down low and go to a nearby diner to use the ladies' room. Clearly, the motel was a far cry from the posh high-rise condo that I had just left in Coconut Grove. *So much for Kevin keeping me safe,* I thought.

While this was not a safe place for me, it certainly was for Kevin: he knew that by parking me there, he was free of worry. No one at the motel would be of interest to me. I had no phone to contact anyone, only a pager. I didn't have access to a car to take off in or even any clue where I was. There was no easy way for me to leave the area surrounding the motel unless Kevin came and picked me up. He'd come by and take me out for a bite to eat. But sometimes he wouldn't show up for days on end. Already he was in complete control of my life.

I stayed at the motel for about three weeks. The longer I stayed, the less safe I felt as I became more aware of the number of crackheads surrounding me. I was now living in their world, and the irony was that I was on drug probation! As I walked down the street in Little Ferry after living there for nearly a month, something clicked and I got the feeling that it was time to get out of there before something terrible happened. I grabbed all my stuff and called a cab from a pay phone and asked the driver to take me someplace safe. "Go to a Bennigan's," I said to the cabbie, figuring that a chain restaurant would at least be in a decent town. He took me to the nearest Bennigan's, but to my dismay it was in an even seedier location than my motel was.

At Bennigan's, I called a car service and told the dispatcher I was lost. A driver arrived and I asked him to take me to the nicest nearby town he could think of. He drove me about thirty minutes to Englewood Cliffs, an upper-middle-class town just across the Hudson River from Manhattan.

In town I walked into a friendly looking neighborhood pizzeria, ordered a couple of slices, took out my notepad and paperwork, and began to regroup. The people who worked at the pizza place were nice and let me sit at a table for as long as I liked and didn't hassle me. After about five hours, Kevin paged me. He asked where I was and I told him. Shortly after, he showed up in a rage to pick me up and caused a huge scene. Much to the other customers' shock and dismay, he dragged me out of the pizza place, threw me into his car, and began to interrogate me as if I were a suspect in one of his FBI cases.

Kevin, paranoid and high on coke, accused me of prostituting myself to the customers and the fellas who worked at the pizza place. I tried to calm him down by explaining that I was there only because I felt unsafe at the motel and simply didn't know where else to go. I told him that I had only a few more weeks in which to renew my probation status in New Jersey, and I had to get settled into a place that seemed acceptable to the court officers. I said that it would be impossible to do that in the sleazebag motel where he had left me.

Unable to accept my reasoning, and without warning, Kevin exploded and punched me in the left side of my face. The blow was powerful and extremely painful. But what was even more painful was that this man who supposedly loved me and had promised to keep me safe had just hit me. As soon as I stood up for myself and my rights, the control freak within Kevin snapped. He couldn't handle it, and he reacted with violence. I was confused, defenseless, and in complete shock.

Now, for most women, this would be a clear red flag to get the hell out of the relationship. However, when you grow up being abused, you don't even know what a warning sign is. I wasn't taught whom or what to stay away from by my parents. I wasn't shown the right way to behave and how others who supposedly love you should behave toward you. Not to mention I was lost. I was alone. I had no home. I had no job. And I didn't know that I was heading into an even darker and more dangerous place than when I'd lived in Florida.

Soon after that incident in the pizzeria parking lot in New Jersey, I moved to New York City and began working nights as an exotic dancer.

Kevin wanted me to get into the business to make money for the both of us. He had admired the way I danced at the nightclubs in Miami and felt I could bring in a significant income as a dancer. He introduced me to a girl named Rosario who worked as an exotic dancer in the city; Rosario had been instructed by Kevin to make me her protégée and teach me how to be successful on the dancing circuit. She lived in a modest apartment in Astoria, Queens, on Nineteenth Street and Ditmars Boulevard. I moved in with her and she began to show me the ropes.

Rosario was a full-figured Puerto Rican. She had a good grasp of the business and how it worked, so I listened to her advice. Rosario taught me many things, including an important survival lesson that stuck with me. "Don't date the customers," she advised. "Never mix business with pleasure."

She brought me to a club called the Baby Doll in Chinatown. I came into the place as Beverly Merrill, auditioned, and was hired. I danced under the name Danielle, in a tiny bikini. I was used to running around all day in Florida in a bikini, so I was comfortable in my "costume." Plus, I was getting paid to do what I loved to do best in Miami—dance.

I didn't have to take my top off, which would not have helped me anyway because I didn't have big boobs back then. Luckily, I didn't need big boobs to make money as a dancer. While everybody was getting fake boobs in the late eighties, I stood out as 100 percent natural, which people found attractive.

Back in those days, nobody could touch me or the other dancers at the strip clubs—it was against the law to have any physical contact between the dancers and the patrons. In fact, the ABC (Alcoholic Beverage Control) was cracking down on many of the strip clubs throughout New York City and taking to jail all the girls who were allowing the customers to touch them or were flashing the patrons. Thankfully, I wasn't working when any of that went down at any of the clubs that employed me. If just one girl broke the law, the authorities shut down the club and took all of the dancers, customers, owners, and managers to jail. Everyone got locked up. Today it seems as if the strip clubs are all about lap dances. Correct me if I'm wrong, but from what I've seen, maybe they should just get a room!

There was no lap dancing back in the day, and touching the dancers was strictly prohibited, so I had no problems with the law. I also had no problem taking a man's entire paycheck every night. They were going to give it to somebody, so why not me? What the guys thought about when they left the club wasn't my concern. I had a bar and a bartender between the patrons and myself, and I collected tips by hand after the guys tossed money at me onstage.

The Baby Doll was a small, dingy club with just a few scattered stages to dance on, each no bigger than a kitchen table. The clientele mostly consisted of bikers who didn't seem to have a lot of money to spend. I knew I wouldn't stick around long. My philosophy was that if I was going to dance, I was going to try to work at the best places so I could make the most money possible.

Soon, I began dancing at a new club near Wall Street in downtown Manhattan. Unfortunately, the clientele was not much more upscale than what I'd dealt with before, even though it was in the heart of the brokerage community. However, one successful and wealthy Japanese doctor who frequented the club a few nights a week took an instant liking to me and began tipping me quite heavily. Little did I know, but another dancer at the club named Lilly was his mistress. When he started taking an interest in me, she quickly let me know about their close relationship: he paid her rent on a $3,000-a-month apartment in Manhattan and dressed her in expensive furs and jewelry. She made it clear that she didn't want to lose her meal ticket and comfy lifestyle to the new girl on the block.

Actually, Lilly didn't have anything to worry about. I let her know right out of the gate that I was not interested in the Japanese doctor in that way—he was just a good customer of mine who paid me well and, for me, that was it. Lilly still didn't like the tips and attention he was giving me and became extremely insecure about it. Sadly, like most dancers in the business, she was working hard but not putting away and saving the money she made. Women like Lilly thought the tips and fast cash were going to last forever. However, I immediately recognized that an exotic dancer had a short shelf life. You need to get in and get out. Saving for a rainy day was absolutely necessary, and I couldn't believe the other girls couldn't see that, too.

I may have been new to the dancing circuit, but I wasn't naive about life or how men think. I saw Lilly's downfall coming a mile away, but clearly she couldn't see the forest for the trees. One night I approached her in the dressing room and said, "He showers you with money, and all you do is blow it shopping. When he leaves you and moves on to a younger girl—which he ultimately will—then you're going to have nothing."

She heard me, but I don't know if she was really listening to the meaning of my message.

The Japanese doctor kept returning to the club and throwing money my way, and one night he took me aside and told me that I had the beauty, ability, and personality to do much better at a more upscale establishment. He suggested that I check out a club called Gallagher's in Long Island City, Queens.

Working at multiple clubs simultaneously wasn't unusual back then. These days, dancers in New York City work at one upscale club, such as a Scores or a Hustler. However, in the eighties, it didn't make sense for a dancer to be working in the same place every single night. Dancers could rotate their schedules by working in as many as twenty different clubs at one time—even state to state—hopping from one to another if they wanted to. Sometimes that meant dancing in two clubs in one day. It was smarter to appear in a club once a week, but no more. This way, customers didn't get bored by seeing you too often or take your presence there for granted. Working on one scheduled night a week at a place made for a more novel experience for the customers, who looked forward to seeing you at their favorite local spot. This kept the experience fresh and kept the men coming back.

I walked into Gallagher's and was immediately met by the manager, Eddie, a big, hulking presence in the place. He took me to see Bruno, the on-site owner. Bruno's office was downstairs by the dressing room, and as we talked, I could see the other gorgeous dancers staring and checking out their new competition—me.

I instantly had a good feeling about the place. The stage was big and impressive. It was clean and rocking, six-deep at the bar, with every stool taken. The huge place was packed, and you could clearly see that everyone working there was making a lot of money. This was the kind of place where I needed to be.

Bruno invited me to go onstage for an audition, and after my performance I got immediately hired. He asked me when I could start. I asked what their strongest night was. He said, "Friday," and I responded, "See you then."

Now that I was dancing at Gallagher's, I decided to step up the showmanship of my game. Costume makers came to the strip clubs several times a week for a few hours a night, taking orders and measuring the girls. Most of the designers were ex-dancers who knew exactly what would attract the customers and turn them on. They also knew the fabrics had to allow us to break them away, yet be durable enough to wear them while dancing hard during our hottest numbers. I began buying custom-made outfits along with the other dancers at the club. Even if the designer used the same fabric for some of the other dancers' outfits, each would have a unique ribbon or unusual hardware attached to make them look different.

I got creative, trying to coordinate my outfits with the themes of my favorite onstage songs. For instance, I'd wear holsters holding water pistols while the DJ played Aerosmith's "Janie's Got a Gun," or I would wear all black for AC/DC's "Back in Black." These outfits cost anywhere between $200 and $400 apiece, but they were well worth the money. The costumes made the performances more like a striptease than just straight dancing and was more theatrical, sexy, and alluring to the customers.

Next, I wanted to learn how to work the pole. One Gallagher's dancer, Cindy, was extremely talented on the pole. She was actually a dancer in the show *Cats* and would come to the club right after the Broadway curtain came down. She had incredible stage presence, and I watched her closely to pick up tips on how to use the pole to my best advantage. From where to hook your legs, to how to go upside down, to how to run, turn, and land in a split, I eventually got it down pat.

In only a few short months, I became a "feature" on the circuit, meaning that I could pick where I wanted to work and what nights suited me. When you're a featured dancer, you get the stage all to yourself. I would do six twenty-minute sets a night. I'd start off with a fast-paced song, go into a medium-paced song, and end with a slow one, reaching a climactic point before I would receive the customers' tips. I danced hard and would be sweating by the end of each set—it was an incredible workout.

I knew how to make good money as an exotic dancer. I was the only dancer in any club—and I was told this often—who would motion to a patron "Just a minute" when he was holding up money for me. I had the presence of mind and confidence to smile and tell guys in the audience to hold on to their money for a minute and not take it from them until I was finished with my dance.

Another trick that I picked up was that making eye contact with each patron was key. I made each man feel as if he were the only one in the world, even if it was for just a brief moment. While looking deep into his eyes, I would seductively roll my hips, turn my body one more time, then move on to the next patron. When I was finished with my set, each and every person was holding up money for me. Whether it was men or women in my audience, it didn't matter. I knew how to turn them on, and I didn't even need to take off all my clothes to do so.

I moved out of Rosario's and into my own apartment in Howard Beach, Queens, where Kevin would come to stay. Although Rosario never made it to work in Gallagher's with me, her advice was right on target at every club I worked in. When men look at a woman onstage in a club, chemistry is involved; a fantasy is created. I've found that a dancer can completely ruin a fantasy by actually giving a man what he's fantasizing about. When that happens, the guy usually gets bored and moves on to a new fantasy. I made sure that my male fans *never* got bored or moved on from me. I never gave them anything beyond seeing me onstage—and that was enough. When men left the club, I remained their true fantasy. To keep that image going, when I left work, I remained aloof and unattainable. I never spoke to or hung out with any of my customers. If they wanted to see me again, they would have to come see me at the club the night I worked. That was it.

One night while I was working at Gallagher's, Lilly, the dancer who was dating the wealthy Japanese man, came into the club on crutches. I hadn't seen her in about three months and heard she hadn't been working for a while. Lilly had fallen and broken her leg and began doing a lot of coke, and her Japanese boyfriend had apparently lost interest in her. I could see that Lilly was upset and out of control, which was not at all how I remembered her being. I was saddened to see her this way, but not surprised, since she ended up dating one of the customers and ruining the fantasy.

When I started working at any new club and befriended the other dancers, I realized that we all had a lot in common. Like me, many had been sexually abused. I would say that over 90 percent of the girls dancing had been abused in some way. This shared experience created a sort of comfort zone for me and, I think, for them, too. Most of the dancers talked openly and honestly about being abused. They would not chat about it nonchalantly, but when it came up and they started talking, it was without too many inhibitions. Sadly, quite a few girls committed suicide because of the abuse that haunted them from their childhoods. The hardest suicide for me to cope with was that of a girl named Gina. She was a beautiful, part Jewish and Italian girl from Brooklyn who was only twenty-two years old who couldn't take the pressure and live with her secret past any longer. The night she died, she overdosed on sleeping pills and a bottle of vodka. She left a suicide note behind, detailing what her father had done to her as a child.

When the coroner established the time of Gina's death, I realized that I had spoken to her just a few hours before. Our conversations were always deep, and we seemed to have a lot in common regarding our pasts, but some women can handle it and some can't, I guess. I am not saying that I am the strongest person in the world, but I can honestly say that the people who have judged me the hardest in my life are those who probably couldn't survive a tenth of what I have gone through. True friends don't judge me, or others, for what has happened in the past; they embrace us for the strength we've conjured to overcome the negatives. After all, we couldn't prevent what occurred. For all I knew, Gina might have met somebody in her life around the time of her death who was tearing her down and not accepting her for her past. On top of her already tortured childhood and tough life, she might have been dealing with somebody who made her feel worse for what had happened. This was the case with many of the dancers I encountered.

Another common thread among the dancers was that most were abused by their boyfriends or husbands at home. Many of the girls came to work with black eyes, bruises, and cuts on their bodies. I was no different from the rest. Curiously, many of us weren't insecure about it. It wasn't as if we were going to the supermarket with a black eye; we were going to a strip club where other women had black eyes, bruised legs, and random cuts. We would help one another cover the bruises with makeup before starting our sets; luckily, the red spotlights that shone down on us and the smoke machines helped hide the black-and-blue marks as well.

The first time Kevin saw me dance, he went nuts with jealousy and told me he wanted me to stop immediately. However, he also wanted me to make money for him. It was a double-edged sword. When he saw how quickly I became successful as a dancer, he was filled with rage. I had no idea that this would be the beginning of a pattern.

I tried to work as often as I could to get away from him. It was my only freedom. I also tried to work in more high-end places, so I could give him just a percentage of what I was making and not all of it. That way, I could put some money away for myself and he would never know. Kevin never questioned me as long as he felt I was giving him what he thought I was making. Plus, if I had given him the full amount I was actually making in high-end places, he would have accused me of selling my body. He accused me of it even when I was giving him just 10 percent of my nightly tips.

After my shift ended, I didn't sit down with my customers to have a drink like some of the other girls. Once in a while I would take five minutes to stand at the bar to say good-bye to everyone, but when I did this, I made sure to have a bouncer next to me. When I said my good-byes, I discovered that my customers were actually charming and quite smart. The more people I had intelligent conversations with at the clubs, no matter how brief they were, the more I realized that I was living a nightmare that I didn't know how to wake up from.

8

SOMEONE TO TALK TO

To say that Kevin and I had an unhealthy relationship couldn't be more of an understatement. The physical and emotional violence made my life a living hell.

When he'd finally come to his senses and realize how much he'd hurt me, he would sometimes attempt to gain control of himself. He would express regret that almost seemed sincere and try to be sweet, calling me his pussycat. What Kevin didn't see on the outside was the emotional battering that he had inflicted on me. Those emotional cuts were even deeper than the physical ones.

During periods of calm in our relationship, Kevin would make an effort to take the medication that seemed to help keep him balanced. It made me realize that he was capable of being civilized when not under the influence of drugs and alcohol. Unfortunately, these moments of peace were few and far between. They would surface and last for only a couple of days, if that, before his demons of addiction would knock on his door and he would answer. Almost without warning, he would drift back into his old out-of-control self. A drink here, a snort of cocaine there, and he was off into a totally unpredictable state of mind, almost like a Dr. Jekyll and Mr. Hyde transformation.

It didn't take much to set him off—it could almost occur with the simple snap of the fingers. The cycle became crystal clear: I was on a roller-coaster ride that I had no idea how to get off of, so I stayed on, naively hoping that things would get better.

All Kevin had mentioned since we first met was the prospect of marrying me. I never understood why he was in such a rush. It was a technique of his to keep me in the picture. I realized soon after we said "I do" that, to him, marriage was more about controlling me than loving me. Kevin's definition of love was ownership, and he wanted to own me. In hindsight Kevin's last name being attached to my name was tied in to his identity in a powerful way, but this was far too complex for me to fully comprehend at the time.

I had always loved the idea of marriage. My relationship with Jorge, who was a wonderful man, should have resulted in our standing at the altar together. However, the timing for both of us was off. I was primed and ready to get married, finally at the point of settling down, but the legal complications ultimately got in the way. Then Kevin came along. I foolishly believed that marriage would change things for the better in our relationship. *Once we get married, Kevin will feel totally secure, and he will be fine,* I thought, with hope in my heart. I would daydream that our marriage would finally make me feel safe and secure as well. I'd have someone standing by my side at all times.

Kevin had his addictions, for sure, but I had mine also. My addiction was the storybook fantasy of love and what it was supposed to feel like. I was more in love with the idea of marriage than I was with Kevin. I think this is a common issue in dysfunctional relationships. I suffered from the delusion that if I married Kevin, then I would finally feel love. I would be Mrs. Maher, and the love I sought would accompany the title *wife.* I imagined that once we got married his insecurities would diminish. He would stop taking drugs and drinking. He would quit obsessing over me. He would make a concerted effort to be a good husband and the supportive man who I had always wanted him to be. Foolishly, I thought we had a shot at normalcy.

Our trip to the altar on October 20, 1988, wasn't exactly what wedding dreams are made of. In fact, it was a nightmare.

Kevin brought his pal Mark, who worked in a car dealership on Long Island, with him to be our witness in front of the justice of the peace. After we said our *I do*'s, Kevin accused me of flirting with Mark. Kevin had come back from the bathroom in the municipal building and didn't like the way Mark was leaning over and talking to me closely.

"I think you offered him sex," he said, his voice filled with jealousy and rage.

"What! You're crazy, Kevin," I said.

"I'm going to show you what happens when you even let another guy talk to you."

We didn't even make it out of the parking lot of the justice of the peace before Kevin lived up to his promise. As soon as I got into the car and looked up from buckling my seat belt, he smashed me in the left side of my face with his fist. My head flew back and hit the passenger-side window, and I blacked out for a brief moment. When I came to, I immediately covered my face as he continued to yell and scream. *This is supposed to be a grown man, my protector, my husband,* I thought. I had thought Kevin would change once we got married, and he did change. He became more brutal and jealous.

I had told my mom about my plans to marry Kevin, and she made it clear that she did not approve. However, as I said, my parents and I did not have a normal relationship, and I never looked for or sought my mom's approval. I always felt I was the stronger one in our mother/daughter relationship. Her opinion of Kevin was correct, of course, but I didn't listen; I was young and thought I knew better. After he hit me the first time, I called my mother and told her what had happened. She told me to get away from him. When I told her I couldn't, she was upset to say the least, but I still thought I knew what I was doing. Women in their early twenties often do, even when they're making big mistakes.

The fight continued back at our apartment as Kevin was high and drunk. I tried to keep to myself as I sat down on the couch nursing my bruised face, while Kevin paced the floor, his nostrils flared, grinding his teeth like an addict. He hadn't slept in a couple of days, which was typical, and his normally bright blue eyes were mere specks within seas of bloodshot red.

That night, Kevin wanted to consummate his marriage to me. I obviously wasn't in the mood. How could I have been? Angry, he told me that I was his wife now and I should show it.

For days, Kevin raged. Terrified for my life, I screamed, cried, begged him to stop the craziness. It's impossible to put into words the feeling of helplessness that I experienced.

Someone eventually called the police for his disturbing the peace, and they eventually arrived and stopped Kevin. I ended up in a hospital bed.

While in the hospital, I was visited by two DEA agents based in Manhattan. They told me that Kevin worked with them, and now that I was his wife, I could be told the truth. I was informed that Kevin wasn't an FBI agent at all. His so-called law enforcement position was as a CI with the FBI.

"What is a CI?" I asked.

The agents told me that CI stands for "confidential informant." A confidential informant is usually a former criminal who assists law enforcement officials by trading inside information and identifying criminal contacts in order to stay out of prison. In street terms, they are basically fucking *rats*. Kevin had been working with the DEA for some time on a case, and they needed to get him out of jail to complete their investigation.

"Wait a second," I said. "He just put me in the hospital and you're asking my permission to get him out of jail? Or are you just announcing to me that you're going to do it?"

"Since you're his wife, we have to tell you," one of the agents responded. "Yes, we're getting him out. We have been working on a case for months and it's finally coming to a head."

"So let me get this straight," I said, trying to comprehend. "Kevin can commit this crime against me because he knows you're going to get him out of jail? I'm not wrong, am I?"

They looked at each other, then turned to me and apologized.

I rolled over, pulled the sheet up over the side of my face, and began to cry. I figured that no matter what Kevin did, he had a get-out-of-jail-free card. He could get high, hit me, get arrested, and walk out of jail just a few hours later. I was in an impossible situation. I had no one to turn to. There was no one to protect me—not even the law. This was only the beginning of my marriage to the "cop without a badge."

––––––––

My probation officer's last name was Fox . . . and let me tell you, it fit him. He'd slyly show up and check on me anytime he wanted to, without any warning. That's what happens when you get arrested and are put in the probation system: the probation officers can show up at any and every hour of the day. But Fox showed up so much at my home not because of me. They were clearly more concerned with my current relationship with Kevin and less concerned with my arrest in Florida. One of the stipulations of probation is to not consort or be associated with any known felons, which I assume is one reason Kevin never told me about his past. The only legal way someone who is on probation can be around a felon is if they are married. Kevin knew this and used it to his advantage. This was why he was in such a rush to marry me. Kevin put me in the worst situation with my probation officers, and I lost credibility with them. Making matters even worse, Kevin would yell at the officers for showing up at our house. There is no way to know for sure, but I think that I would have finished my probation earlier if I hadn't been involved with Kevin.

When I first met Kevin back in Florida, he constantly told me about how he could help make my arrest and punishment easier, but in the end I think our involvement made it much more difficult for me. I had already gotten probation due to my plea bargain, so what did he actually achieve for me? What was the great business that he encouraged me to get into? Stripping. When on probation, you aren't allowed to serve alcohol or even be around that stuff, and there I was, working in an atmosphere that was totally conducive to abusing drugs and alcohol. The owners of the clubs and bars had to get special permission to allow me to work there since I was on probation. They went out on a limb for me, fully knowing that the authorities were going to watch over them even more closely—that was how much money I was making for them—and probation officers actually started coming to the strip clubs to check on me. I guess in their eyes I was a draw and worth the extra hassle.

Many of the other dancers at the clubs were doing drugs and alcohol, and I saw them make bad decision after bad decision as a result. I believe that my being on probation forced me to make better choices and stay on a less risky track. Following through with a drug rehab program was mandatory with my arrest. My Judgment and Probation Commitment Order, filed on November 19, 1986, outlined specific orders that I had to comply with during my five-year probation, including participating in a drug treatment program and getting tested for drugs during my first six months on probation.

I was under a strict court order not to do any drugs or consume any alcohol during my probation. I was tested and checked constantly, at specific times and even randomly at my home.

I had to do a mandatory urinalysis every three days because it takes seventy-two hours to get certain drugs out of your system. For instance, it takes two to three days to get cocaine out of your system. For a heavy user who is constantly doing the drug, it can take up to two to three weeks to be clear. Marijuana can take up to eight weeks to disappear from your system. When you are assigned to a rehab program, you can't beat the system.

I peed in more cups and in more locations than you can

imagine. I got so good at it that I could have peed into a salt-shaker and not miss a single drop. Officers would come into the bathroom with me since, at the time, people on parole were reportedly taping bags of other people's urine to their legs. The stories were true: I had past offenders offer me money for my drug-free urine. (The technology back in the eighties was not what it is today; now they know whether the urine is yours or not.)

The authorities verified that I was doing what the law required and was free and clear of drugs and alcohol. A letter dated December 6, 1988, to Judge Eugene Spellman of the U.S. District Court in the Southern District of Florida from Deborah Como of the Counseling Service of EDNY, Inc., located in Brooklyn, New York, described my drug-free status:

> *I am writing you on behalf of Beverly Merril* [sic] *who has been a client at the above Substance Counseling Service since 10/2/87. Since this time she has been coming very regularly for weekly individual counseling sessions and group therapy. In conjunction with treatment, she has been given twice weekly urine monitoring. They have all come up negative i.e., no trace of illicit drugs or alcohol.*

The drug treatment program I was sentenced to attend met at nine o'clock every Wednesday night in Brooklyn. When I first walked into the room and saw the mishmash of unfortunate people there, I immediately thought, *What am I doing here? This is not me!* The members of this all-women's group were from all walks of life—stockbrokers, housewives, bikers, lesbians—and we'd all sign in and sit around in a circle. The drill was to first let everyone know how you ended up in the rehab program. Then, when the introductions were finished, we were invited to talk freely about the problems and circumstances that had brought each of us there. When it came time for you to talk, you could either speak or say a simple "Pass." At any pause or moment of silence in the participants' input, anyone in the group could take the floor and announce that he or she had something to discuss; the participants never interrupted one another. Listening to the various stories, I was surprised at how bright and intelligent, yet deeply troubled, many of the people were.

Even though we all looked different and were from various social backgrounds, we had one problem in common—we were all addicted to something. I found out another thing I had in common with some of them: many of the people in treatment had been sexually abused during their childhoods, just as I had been. The stories didn't end when the meetings finished. Many nights, I drove members of the group home to Manhattan, Queens, and Brooklyn, listening during the ride to additional stories of their woes. We became like members of a family, which added to the strength and newfound confidence that was developing in each of us.

I checked into the program thinking that I had no real addictions, that I was just there to fulfill my probation requirements. I didn't have any expectations about what the program would do for me. After all, I wasn't an alcoholic. I wasn't using drugs. Did I? Well, yes, I did. I enjoyed partying during my youth. Who doesn't? However, the experience I went through in Florida was enough to get me to quit even the most casual use of party favors. I recognized problems in the other group members when I saw them, and at first I convinced myself that I was the most normal member of the support group.

While many of the other people in the program had addictions that were clearly visible on the surface, mine were buried more deeply. After spending weeks and months at these sessions talking to the people in the group about my past abuse as well as my current relationship, the real problems within me began to rise to the surface. I realized that I did have addictions like everyone else. However, they were not of the drug/alcohol variety. Mine consisted of codependency and enabling, which can be just as—or even more—self-destructive as a substance-abuse problem.

It has always been in my nature to help others, probably because no one truly helped me during my childhood or in my young adult life. Even though I was living a chaotic personal life much of the time—especially during my years immediately after the trial—I still seemed to find the time to help others who appeared to be worse off than I was. When you care about people and they are down-and-out, especially if they are battling depression and an addiction to drugs or alcohol, you want to help them through it any way you can. However, Kevin taught me that helping people is not always the most positive thing you can do for them.

Many times I would try to calm Kevin's anger and get him to a reasonable, normal state. What I should have done was lock him out of the house and out of my life. In fact, in all of my serious relationships I enabled them to continue their ways while I supported them emotionally, financially, etc., etc., etc. It gets exhausting and you lose yourself and your identity in the process, causing an onslaught of problems for yourself.

My theory now is if there are no consequences for bad behavior then the bad behavior continues and multiplies. It goes along with boundaries that I needed to set. If I had been more clear about mine with no fear, then I wouldn't have allowed them to be crossed by every partner I had. I would have set my bar much higher, which is in essence exactly what I do now. Often, I would make excuses for Kevin's outlandish and uncontrollable behavior to whoever would ask me, "Why are you with him?" I would also come to his rescue. I kept giving him another shot, another chance, at having a relationship with me—clear signs of being an enabler who was losing a grip on things and not willing to face the realities at hand. So make no excuses. Instead, set boundaries.

Even though I couldn't see it then, I was in a classic codependent relationship. Codependency is continuing to interact and be with someone when you are in a clearly dysfunctional relationship with that person, and it has been documented that codependency and enabling go hand in hand. People who have these characteristics stay in bad relationships, and this can be traced to roots in bigger problems in their lives. Since I knew practically no one in New York City prior to my arrival, and Kevin had brought me there, I was codepending on him for survival. I wasn't my own person or in control of my life, and I was losing my identity more and more every day.

Additionally, I had severe self-esteem issues stemming from my childhood that were the basis of my relationship problems with men. I didn't realize that I deserved better. The women in my group therapy sessions became a center of strength for me. When they would ask me for my opinion and advice, it made me feel needed, significant, and important. I was a vital participant within that group, which to me symbolized family—in essence, the first family I ever had, albeit a family of misfits, but my family. They helped me realize that I deserved better than my current situation and much more from a partner in my life.

Once in the program, you could miss a certain number of the sessions, but I never missed one. I loved to hear about the participants' experiences and enjoyed sharing mine with them. It was my only chance to talk to anyone openly and honestly about my life. As I got stronger with the help of my support group, Kevin began to notice a distinct change in me. I began to separate myself from him and relished the moments of personal freedom when he was out of the picture, working. He would sometimes leave for days, even weeks, to conduct his various assignments. I discovered later that while I thought

Kevin was busy with his assignments, he was also spying on me, using surveillance equipment, because he was certain that I was cheating on him. So I guess *I* was an undercover case. While my feelings for Kevin had begun to deteriorate, no other guy was in my life. I wouldn't subject another man to the craziness. I was simply getting stronger on my own, something he didn't think I was capable of.

When Kevin started to believe that I'd gained my independence and the strength to leave the relationship, he freaked out, and in one drunken outburst threatened to plant drugs in my car, then call the authorities and have me sent back to prison in Florida. While I didn't think he'd do that sober, when he was high or drunk, who knew? I was the only person I knew free of alcohol and drugs that was in a constant state of paranoia.

9

ЅEND ME AN ANGEL

Throughout the rehab and the domestic disturbances, I developed quite a following as an exotic dancer. Eventually, I created a four-by-six postcard detailing my steady schedule of appearances, which I would hand out to customers. On one side was a listing of the days, times, and various clubs that I would be appearing at in New York and New Jersey, and on the other side was a dramatic photograph of me from behind wearing only a thong and stilettos.

One evening I went in to work at Gallagher's as I normally did, pleased to get out of the house and ready to dance. I worked as much as I could, since if I wasn't dancing, I would have been forced to spend my nights with Kevin.

Kevin carried a badge on him, which he would flash around,

pretending he was a cop or FBI or DEA agent, depending on what the situation called for. People didn't understand how he could flash a badge one moment and then be snorting cocaine with them the next. There was no cop in Kevin. He was a fake cop. Fake FBI agent. Fake DEA agent. But he was a real *rat*.

The owners of the clubs I worked at disliked Kevin. He would walk into a place as if he owned it, and they all despised the way he bullied me.

That evening, the lights shone brightly as I danced onstage. Then, through the sea of people, I spotted Kevin harassing the bouncer at the front door of the club. Thoughts of Kevin's outbursts and threats descended on me in a flash, and I realized that when someone is obsessed, no restraining order or any other legally backed piece of paper in the world can shield you from him or her. Suddenly the bouncers, bartenders, and club owner began rushing toward the stage to protect me. In the meantime, Kevin went out to his Porsche in the parking lot, then returned to the club with a gun.

With nostrils flared and pupils dilated in what I imagine was a cocaine-induced fury, Kevin pushed his way into the club, armed and dangerous. The other dancers and I were immediately rushed downstairs to the dressing room to protect us from the man I called my husband. Somehow Kevin broke loose from one of the big, tattooed bouncers. Even in my shock I was amazed that these bouncers were risking their lives for me; I was at such a low point in my life that *I* wouldn't even have risked my life for me.

Once the dancers and I were safe inside, Eddie, one of the managers, blocked the dressing room door. Kevin put a gun right up to Eddie's head. Eddie knew Kevin and, more important, knew his reputation for going overboard when he was drunk and sky-high. Still, Eddie looked Kevin dead in the eye and didn't back down.

From behind the closed door, my mind was racing as I listened to the bizarre scene unfolding outside. Inside, everyone was freaking out; not many of the dancers had seen guns like that before.

Before Kevin had time to accept Eddie's challenge, the police finally arrived. The officers approached Kevin to calm him down. He assaulted one of the officers, and they arrested him and wouldn't let him go. It was rather ironic to me that only when Kevin assaulted another man—a man who carried a gun and could defend himself—did they finally press charges against him. I thought about the times Kevin had hurt me and I'd ended up in the hospital, and how even though he'd hurt me—a defenseless woman—they always let him go. It was extremely unfair. While I was grateful that they were pressing charges, I couldn't understand why I wasn't able to do the same.

The police offered me a ride down to the station. When one of the detectives was filling out the report, I told him my full name. They paused, confusion blanketing their faces. "If you are Mrs. Maher, then who is the other woman in the station?" one of the detectives asked.

"What other woman?" I shot back.

Kevin's other wife, Beth Maher—who I believed was his ex-wife—came down to the jail. I found out later from Kevin that he'd married Beth under the name Edward James Maher, and he married me under Kevin James Maher—*while he was still legally married to another woman.* At that moment I found out Kevin was a bigamist.

Shocked, I immediately walked out of the precinct.

I found out later that Beth resided in New Jersey, and Kevin helped lock up her previous husband, the father of her son. Kevin preyed upon Beth—much the same way he preyed upon me.

After the incident at the club, I quickly moved to Brooklyn and left no trail. However, it didn't take Kevin long to find me. One day, out of the blue, he showed up on my doorstep, claiming that he had broken up with Beth. In truth, she had ended it with him. He also said that he had stopped using. It was a familiar story, but for some reason I bought into it one last time.

Kevin wanted to get back together with me and suggested that we move to the Poconos in Pennsylvania for a change of lifestyle and a fresh start. It wasn't as if we had many choices of places where we could live, and the landlords in the Poconos were not exactly discerning. Our track record as tenants was pretty pathetic: we had moved eight times in a year and a half because we were kicked out of so many apartments and two-family homes in the tristate area. The problem was never that the rent was unpaid. *I* always paid it on time and in full. But we were always fighting loudly and violently, which, plus the occasional visits from the police, prompted several landlords to ask us to leave. They were sick and tired of trouble. Therefore, getting a reference from any of our previous landlords was not an option.

The gated community that we moved to was called the Pocono Country Place. Visitors had to go through a security checkpoint to get inside—this was a world away from where we had lived in the various boroughs of New York City—and the development was popular among families from Staten Island and Brooklyn, who could buy or rent vacation homes. The Pocono Country Place was equally busy in the warm months as in the cold; it manufactured snow that covered mountains in the winter and boasted a manmade lake with a beach for the summer.

I paid $1,400 a month to rent a simple yet pretty home for us. The houses were all brand-new, with tons of property and a great deal of privacy. You couldn't even see your neighbors' homes. With this move, it seemed as if Kevin and I had finally achieved some peace of mind. *Maybe this is what we needed,* I thought. *Maybe things will get normal.*

Soon after we moved, I began working again at two different strip clubs: Shakers in Carlstadt and Satin Dolls in Lodi, both of which were in New Jersey. (Satin Dolls eventually became famous as the Bada Bing! club in the hit television series *The Sopranos*.)

The major difference between the exotic dance clubs in New York City and New Jersey is that New York City is topless and New Jersey is not. I disliked being topless. In the city, I often got into trouble because many times I didn't want to take my top off. Even when I did take it off, I often had pasties on, which was something you weren't supposed to do. The money was more or less the same, so going to dance in New Jersey was a welcome change.

Kevin would take me to work in his Porsche, driving all the way down Route 80 from the Poconos. Kevin started using drugs and drinking again shortly after we settled in. He became obsessed with every moment of my day and my total existence, going so far as to follow me into the bathroom. Then Kevin became fixated on the idea of my having a baby with him. It was just like when he was preoccupied with wanting to marry me—he wouldn't take no for an answer. Getting me pregnant was all that he talked about. It seemed like just another way to control me.

The last thing I wanted to do was have a baby with Kevin, and I did my best not to. There is no foolproof means of birth control, but I was trying everything within my power to get my body to reject pregnancy. His obsession with me was only getting worse. As much as I dreamed of being a mother, bringing a child into our relationship would have been the ultimate crime.

Since I wasn't getting pregnant, Kevin insisted we go to an ob-gyn to find out what the problem was with me. On examining me, the doctor didn't see anything wrong with my reproductive system, but he did see a battered woman.

Kevin wouldn't let me go into the examination room alone with the doctor, even though a nurse was present. He was completely paranoid. Kevin told the doctor that if I didn't get pregnant it would be the doctor's fault, and that if I went to see the doctor by myself and ended up getting pregnant, Kevin would think that the doctor was the father. In one breath he was asking the doctor for his professional help, and in the next breath he was accusing the doctor of having an affair with me. During one visit I said I was having bad menstrual cramps and had the nurse escort me to the bathroom. In reality I was creating an opportunity to get a message to the doctor through her that I didn't want to have a baby with Kevin. After our conversation, she agreed to help me.

"You should come to our office every day," the nurse said.

"Why?" I asked.

"Because we can give you a birth control pill every day if you come here." She knew that if the doctor prescribed me birth control pills and Kevin found them, he'd be infuriated.

Per their advice, I stopped at the doctor's office every day to get birth control pills. Kevin assumed that I was getting hormone injections to help me get pregnant. The doctor was giving me a combination of shots in my butt, but they were B_{12} for energy as well as saline.

During my doctor visits, my trips to the bathroom with the nurse became more frequent. She began relating ways that I could escape from my relationship; she told me about support groups that could help me and said that if I came to their medical office alone, she and her husband would take me to the group meetings. I wished I had had the courage to go.

Things between Kevin and me got progressively worse. He took off at one point for a few days—for work or on a coke binge, I had no idea. It was a welcome relief, but I was waiting for the ball to drop.

———

Once, after I finished work at about 2:00 a.m., I drove back to the Poconos. When I entered the Pennsylvania side of Route 80, I looked in my rearview mirror and noticed Kevin tailing me. He began to follow me aggressively, and after a frightening cat-and-mouse chase on the highway, we both arrived home. I locked myself in the car and Kevin banged extremely hard on the window. I was terrified he would break the glass, causing us both bodily harm and enraging him further. I relented and unlocked the door, and he dragged me into the house. Kevin threw me down on the bed and said, "If you just make love to me, I'll stop."

Make love to him? I thought. Making love to Kevin was the furthest thing from my mind. My mind was twisting and turning. *Would it be easier to just give Kevin what he wants?* I thought. I gave in and stopped fighting it. During it, I began to cry—not the type of cry where you are bawling out loud. It was the kind of cry that you are not letting anyone know about. And yet, I was face-to-face with the person causing me to be upset. When it was all done, I put my back to him as I rolled over. Then I heard sobbing sounds. As I turned I noticed Kevin was sitting on the floor crying and looking at me apologetically. He kept telling me how beautiful I was, then asked, "Why do I keep hurting you? Why do I keep doing this? Help me. Please help me. I need your help."

Although I didn't know the exact psychological term, I thought Kevin suffered from a split personality disorder. *I have to keep him from turning back into that other deranged person,* I thought as he kept rambling on and on.

"If we just had a baby together," Kevin pleaded, "then everything would be okay. Please." At that moment I realized that I might have a chance to end this destructive relationship. While Kevin was in his apologetic and sedate state, I decided to take a shot and let him know that we were finished. I simply couldn't be with him anymore. I was crying as I told him our relationship was over.

Amazingly, Kevin seemed okay with it. He actually said that he was going to leave the house.

Really? That almost seemed too easy, I thought as it made me suspicious. I had never imagined that all I had to do was wait until he was on the timid side of one his mood swings and he would just leave. Before he left the house, Kevin said he had to go to the bathroom; a couple of minutes later I heard heavy sniffing going on inside. Kevin was snorting coke—big-time.

When Kevin came out of the bathroom, he immediately took me by the back of my neck and threw me up against the wall.

I prayed for an angel to hear me, because nobody else was going to hear my screams in the wilderness. The peaceful and isolated home that I had thought might change our relationship for the better turned out to be the most dangerous place I could have been in.

10

THE LA/T DANCE

Ring, ring, ring . . .

I could hear the phone in the kitchen of our Poconos home, but I didn't have the strength to answer it. I could barely move. I was lying on the floor near the staircase, terrified and in severe pain.

The brawl that had been going on for hours between Kevin and me had finally reached a time-out. Kevin was sitting on the floor nearby, confused. This was, of course, a now-familiar pattern to me—he would come on like a crazed animal and exhaust himself by beating the hell out of me. Then he would usually sit there crying, telling me how sorry he was, claiming that he couldn't understand why he did these terrible things to me. But this time he wasn't saying anything at all. Kevin just stared straight ahead with a blank look on his face.

The police arrived and tried to enter the house a few times by knocking on the front door, but to no avail. Eventually they went to the back sliding-glass door, and they could see through the window that the house was in disarray. They forced their way in and discovered me at the bottom of the steps. I didn't have the strength to say much, but they could tell that I was pretty beaten up. They asked me who did it to me and I told them that it was my husband.

Kevin was still sitting near me in a daze when the police arrived. He admitted to the authorities what he had done. What choice did he have but to confess? From the way I looked, it was clear what had happened. Kevin was put in handcuffs and was cooperative with the cops—a much calmer scene compared to the time that he was arrested at Gallagher's.

The officers helped me to my feet. Suddenly I heard my name called out by my mother: "Beverly!" At first I thought I was imagining things. Then my mom appeared before me with my cousin Barbara, who was quite a bit older than me. She immediately wrapped her arms around me, so happy to find I was still alive.

My mother had been phoning the house, trying to reach me. She had become extremely concerned because she hadn't heard from me in a few days because, the last time we spoke, I had told her that things weren't going well between Kevin and me. Mom was aware of Kevin's violent behavior, and my silence and her intuition about what it meant had prompted her to jump in the car and come to my rescue.

While they were driving en route, Mom and Barbara had kept stopping and calling my house from pay phones, desperately trying to contact me. But I wasn't answering. Along the way, they checked the clubs where I had been working and learned that I hadn't been seen in days. Mom was extremely worried and feared the worst, so she called the local police.

While Kevin was put in the back of a police car, I was put in the back of an ambulance and taken to the nearest Pennsylvania hospital. I spent a couple of days recovering from a concussion and assorted contusions. My cuts and lacerations didn't require stitches, but my head was pretty banged up. The hospital did various CAT scans on me and conducted several blood tests; the doctors discovered my blood pressure was dangerously low and monitored me for a few days.

When I got out of the hospital, my mom decided that I should stay at her home for a while to regroup. When my mom finally divorced my dad, I wanted to help her so I bought her a modest home in Jamestown, New York, a small town close to Buffalo and known for being the birthplace of Hollywood legend Lucille Ball. My mother had since settled into her life there and was quite happy. She was working as an insurance agent and lived a modest but fulfilling life.

When I arrived in the town, located at the heart of a snow belt, it was winter with subzero temperatures, but everyone who lived there shared a closeness. On Sundays, we'd all pile into a house the size of my living room to watch a football game. The women weren't catty and the men didn't treat me like a piece of meat. Nobody was flashy. Everyone would just throw on a pair of jeans and snow boots—not Burberry or Gucci boots, just boots—and go about his or her business. It was a nice change of pace and the perfect place for me to finally get some much-needed rest and relaxation.

One night, I came home from a local pub with a group of friends. When we pulled up to my mom's house, she ran outside, panic-stricken. She pulled me into the house and said, "He was here!"

Kevin had a restraining order against him. Maybe he thought that since I was now in New York State and not Pennsylvania it couldn't be enforced.

My mom told me she had taken care of the situation. I didn't ask her any questions. I didn't want to ask questions. My mom had taken care of me—her daughter. It was rare for me to relinquish all control, but I was exhausted and gave in.

After some time, I left Jamestown and headed back to New Jersey. I moved into an apartment with a couple of friends in Parsippany. My next step was to divorce Kevin. I didn't think Kevin was going to sign divorce papers, so my attorney advised me to file for divorce due to abandonment, which didn't require Kevin's signature. He informed me that if you're seeking divorce on the grounds of abandonment, you have to make it seem as

if you're actively looking for your spouse, so we ran a "missing person" ad in the local newspaper every day for eighteen
months. With Kevin in jail, the plan worked.

I started dancing again and was making good money. I
moved into my own place and things finally started looking
up. One afternoon while working at Shakers, I met a customer
named Tom. I didn't pay him much attention, but I must've
certainly caught his eye because he tipped me extremely well.
The next afternoon he came back, and the day after that and
the day after that.

Tom had sandy blond hair, blue eyes, and looked to be in
his thirties. He told me he was recently divorced with no children. He worked in the area and would come to Shakers on his
lunch break. Tom was a successful businessman; along with his
brother, Jerry, he owned and ran a lucrative family business that
manufactured the best-selling in-home treadmill unit in the
world. Tom made a good living, to say the least.

Tom began coming to the club more and more often
and giving me expensive gifts—TAG Heuer watches, diamond
rings in the shape of the letter *D* in script, and other lavish
items. The other dancers saw how Tom treated me and tried to
make their own moves on him, but he would brush them aside.
His focus was on me.

Tom told me that he fell in love with me at first sight. *Love?
More like lust,* I thought. Even though I wasn't really buying it,
he did seem genuine. Tom wanted to take me out on a date,

but he was a customer and I didn't want to go there. Plus, for the first time in a long time I wasn't in a relationship, and I was enjoying my newfound freedom.

While the abandonment papers were being processed, I went to therapy. During my probation, I went to group counseling, but I'd never attended a one-on-one session. I knew I had a lot of unresolved issues in my life, and I realized that I needed to work on myself before I could be good for anyone else.

While in therapy, one of the issues I tackled head-on was my previous nineteen marriage engagements. When I talked about being engaged nineteen times on *The Real Housewives of New Jersey,* people immediately jumped to conclusions and thought, *Oh, my God, Danielle slept with all of those men!* Did I have sex with some of them? Absolutely. Did I sleep with all nineteen? Absolutely *not.* Some of these men asked me to marry them after just one kiss. Some after just two dates. For me, it was all a big, twisted game—a contest within myself to see how fast these men would ask me to marry them and put a ring on my finger.

Looking back, these nineteen men loved me enough to marry me and spend the rest of their lives with me. In return, I took a major chunk of their hearts, ripped them out, and stomped all over them. I didn't stop there. I allowed these guys to take me home to meet their families, even though I knew that

I had no intention of marrying them. Their mothers would ask me a series of questions, mainly regarding devotion, dedication, and wifely duties, and I would always respond enthusiastically. I told them anything they wanted to hear to secure their blessings, and once I got the ring, I handed it back to the guys and said, "Bye-bye." It was a sick cycle and a nasty thing for me to do. I'm not proud of it. I wasn't proud of it back then. I was just caught up in it.

Through therapy, I realized that my putting these men through this rejection and heartbreak was a direct result of my being sexually abused as a child. I felt that by hurting these men, I was punishing the past abusers. But what I didn't realize was that I wasn't punishing anyone except myself and these innocent young men who were falling in love with me. I wanted to see them suffer. I wanted them to feel pain. That's what made me feel good, until it didn't feel good any longer. I don't remember what triggered me to stop this horrible behavior, but one day something clicked and I realized that what I had been doing was terribly wrong. Although I didn't understand yet why I was doing it, I did have an epiphany of sorts. That was the beginning of my realization that you need to do unto others as you see fit for yourself.

I decided during therapy that it might be healthy to seek out some of these men. I wanted to apologize for hurting them, and hopefully we could both have some closure. Over the next few months, I made attempts to locate many of them and made a lot of trips to Canarsie and Mill Basin—predominantly Jewish sections of Brooklyn, because I dated mostly Jewish men. Jewish men were attentive and treated women extremely well. They also didn't like girls who quickly jumped into bed with them, which worked well for me. They all also seemed to appreciate that I was pretty, lively, and fun. Sure, I was different from what their Jewish parents might have had in mind for their sons. But as soon as Mom and Dad got to know me and I told them that I was willing to convert to Judaism, they quickly fell in love with me, too.

When I finally located and met with some of these men from my past, I'd tell them with genuine remorse I was sorry. Some accepted my apology. Others were standoffish. And then there was Robert.

Robert and I had dated for quite some time. He was a great guy and I would have been wise to stay with him. Robert was attractive, successful, and would have taken care of me for the rest of my life. But I didn't love him the way he loved me. When I broke up with Robert, I not only gave him back the engagement ring, I also gave him back all the jewelry he ever bought for me. I felt it was the right thing to do. I wanted him to move on, and in a way, by breaking up with Robert, I did him a favor: I gave him the chance to find true love.

When I met with Robert to apologize for what I had done to him, he told me that he was seriously dating someone. I was happy to hear that. But soon after our brief meeting, he called me up and said my sudden reappearance in his life had rekindled a lot of emotions inside him, and he realized that he was still in love with me. He broke up with his girlfriend and wanted to marry me. *Uh-oh. Here we go again,* I thought.

Robert started coming to the clubs I worked at to tell me that I didn't have to dance anymore, that he would marry me and take me away from this life. What he didn't understand—and many men didn't—was that I liked dancing and making my own money.

In an effort to get him to stop holding out hope, I explained to Robert that my coming to see him wasn't about getting back together, it was about me making right all the wrong I had done to others—*do unto others as you would have others do unto you.* I told him that he was crazy to want to jump back into a relationship with me and advised him to figure out why he would want to be with me after I had already hurt him so badly. I asked him, why would he want something or someone in his life capable of doing that? He seemed confused and couldn't answer me, but I think he finally got the point.

While meeting up with the men from my past was a good step toward clearing my own conscience, I began to think that maybe it wasn't good for some of the guys. *Maybe it's better to let it be,* I thought. I realized that seeking out these men from my past should, in fact, be a thing of the past. I needed to start living in the present. And the present was finally beginning to look good. I had my freedom and also a new man in my life who treated me well on all levels, even though I was keeping him at arm's length. It was certainly not something I was used to, but could get used to for sure.

During this time, I wasn't pushing Tom away entirely. I honestly kept telling him that he could do better and that I wasn't right for him. And I wasn't. But that intrigued Tom even more. A lot more.

Taking things slowly with Tom was good not only for me but for him. Let's face it, he met me in a strip club. I needed to make sure that I wasn't just Tom's fantasy onstage, but was his fantasy in real life. I had also just gotten out of a dysfunctional marriage and was still on probation. On paper, I wasn't exactly ideal wife material. I was honest and told Tom that I wasn't the type of girl you bring home to Mom. His response took me by surprise: "You're exactly the kind of girl that I'd bring home to my mom." Clearly, he wasn't going to give up.

In truth, by keeping Tom at a distance, I was testing his feelings. Amazingly, he continued to pass with flying colors.

———

For a year and a half, Tom consistently courted me. Even though he showed me tons of attention, tipped me extremely well, and never so as much as glanced at any of the other dancers in the club, I felt our relationship was business, not pleasure, and remained reluctant to cross the line. Despite his advances, I continued to keep my distance as best I could. Tom wasn't allowed to call me or visit my home—he didn't even have my address or phone number. He knew my schedule, though, and would visit me at work almost every day.

When the DJ ended the music and I was done with my set, I would often talk with Tom after I left the stage. Chatting with him from behind the bar kept a comfortable distance between us. I worried that at any moment Kevin would burst through the doors of the club, see Tom and me together, and lose control. Staying on opposite sides of the bar kept both of us safe. I found it refreshing that Tom, who was an extremely busy businessman, chose to sit at the bar for hours to be able to talk to me for five minutes. That intrigued me. He was different from anyone else I had ever met, which intrigued me even more.

Tom kept asking me to go out on a date with him and I kept turning him down. There is something to be said for persistence, though. While I was difficult to get close to, Tom eventually found my weakness: sushi.

I *adored* sushi. (I still do!) Through our long talks at the club, I found out that Tom had never eaten sushi before. Here was a well-educated man who could buy himself anything, had traveled around the world many times over, and yet I could still teach him something: how to eat sushi. I found this interesting, and Tom was happy to indulge me.

Tom and I went on our first date to Kiku, a Japanese restaurant on Route 4 in Paramus, New Jersey. When we met in the parking lot, he told me to wait a minute before we went inside. Then he opened the trunk of his car and pulled out a motorized scooter. He started it up, hopped on, and took a joyride around the parking lot. *Look at this guy!* I thought as I pointed and laughed. I didn't know what to think of this grown man riding around on a little scooter like a teenager. Bear in mind that this was the late eighties and nobody had motorized scooters back then. But Tom was like James Bond, always acquiring all of the coolest and newest gadgets. It was endearing and supercute. However, a much deeper message was being conveyed: Tom wanted to show me that he wasn't just some guy in a bar. He was different. Tom had a quirky, fun, childlike side of him that he wanted to share with me. I have to admit, it worked.

While I taught Tom how to eat sushi that night, he taught me a few things, too. He taught me how to feel safe again. He taught me how to have a normal relationship again. He taught me how to laugh again. He taught me how to love again.

One dinner date turned into two, three, four, five, and I eventually lost count in a sea of wasabi and soy sauce. Then, dinner dates at night turned into lunch dates in the afternoon. Tom even began joining me during my shopping excursions to Nordstrom. Gwen, my personal shopper, was a little taken aback when one day Tom reached in his wallet and gave her a credit card while I was in the dressing room. He told her from then on to put everything I bought on his card.

While I thought it was sweet of him to offer to pay my bill, I wasn't looking for a sugar daddy. I didn't need one. I was happy making my own money, paying my own bills, and being an independent woman, so when I emerged from the dressing room, I told Tom thanks, but no thanks. Later on, I found out that in doing so I had hurt his feelings. The next time I saw

Gwen at Nordstrom, she set me straight: "Tom is a really nice guy. He doesn't want to buy you clothes to impress you. He knows you have the money to pay for them. He just wants to do something nice for you because he knows you love to shop. Let him do this for you. Let him be the man."

The experience taught me that sometimes you do have to let a man be a man. And boy, did Tom enjoy being the man! He couldn't buy me enough stuff. Every day a new designer outfit arrived at my doorstep. This was a big change of pace for me. I went from giving the money that I made to a man, to a man giving me more than any woman could need. Was this payback for all the pain I went through in a loveless marriage? I wasn't sure, but as far as I was concerned, it felt pretty damn good.

Tom took good care of me. I didn't have to work anymore, but I liked to dance and continued to do so. I didn't mind sharing my life with Tom, but I wasn't about to give up my identity. I was a dancer and he was well aware of that. He didn't push me to leave the business, but was happy to support me if I wanted that, so while he focused on making all the right moves in our relationship, I continued to make my moves on the dance floor.

One night at work, the manager at Shakers told me that he had heard that Kevin was out of prison. Worried for my safety, Tom offered to follow me home from work. I told him that I would be fine, but he insisted, and I finally gave in and told him okay. *Let the man be the man,* I thought.

Once we pulled up in front of my place, I waved Tom over to my car. He parked and walked over to the window of my Porsche. Using my finger, I told him to come closer . . . closer . . . closer. Then I kissed him passionately. That was our first kiss.

The next evening, Tom and I went out to dinner. He got down on one knee and asked me if I would marry him. I said yes.

"I can't wait to knock you up!" he exclaimed, which I thought was kind of cute.

"It would help if we had sex first," I responded, as I hadn't yet done anything more than kiss Tom. We both laughed, then Tom gave me a pre-engagement ring, which had a five-carat diamond. It would soon be followed by a seven-carat ring.

I started crying. Finally, after all the pain I endured, happy tears rolled down my face.

I couldn't believe that I was going to marry Tom. We were so different! Tom was well-educated, while I was street-smart. His upbringing was relatively normal, while mine was any-thing but. He had designer suits in his closet, while I had skel-etons in mine. He was the kind of guy parents dream about and hope their daughters marry. I was a parent's nightmare. However, it seemed that while I was finally looking for some-thing more grounded in my life, Tom wanted to take a walk on the wild side.

I guess opposites *do* attract.

Even though I was engaged to Tom, I continued to work

on the strip-club circuit. I still enjoyed being the center of attention onstage. The lights, the crowd, the music—it was a high that I wasn't ready to come down from just yet. Plus, the money I was making wasn't too bad, either.

One night at Shakers, as the music ended and I finished my set, I collected the money off the stage as usual. Out of the corner of my eye I saw a five-dollar bill being offered across the bar in my direction. I reached out and put my hand on the bill and said, "Thank you." The customer slapped his hand on top of mine, startling me, and didn't let go. I immediately looked up and, to my shock and surprise, I was face-to-face with Kevin. Staring intently, he told me that this time he wasn't going to let me go.

I pulled away and ran back to the dressing room. I didn't want to leave the club alone that night. Someone drove my car home and I left with another dancer, Missy, and spent the night at her apartment in Hoboken. When I arrived at Missy's, I called Tom and told him what had happened. I let him know that I was leaving for Florida in a few days to hide out. Ironically, Florida was the safest spot for me to hide until the abandonment papers went through. I didn't think Kevin would ever imagine that I would go back there.

Over the next few days, I planned my trip down south. I called my probation officer and alerted him that I would be heading to Florida. While they weren't crazy about my leaving the state, they understood, considering the circumstances.

I stopped by the bank and took out some money. I alerted my friends in Fort Lauderdale that I was coming back to town to hide.

Once again I was running from my past, praying it wouldn't catch up with me.

I got into my Porsche and drove from New York City to Virginia. I put my car on the auto train and seventeen hours later got off in Kissimmee, Florida. Then I drove another five hours to Fort Lauderdale, where I checked into the Marriott Harbor Beach Hotel, right on the water. I got a huge penthouse suite and lived on room service and takeout. After I'd been there for two weeks, Tom came down and gave the front desk a credit card and paid for the whole thing. He didn't stay long, but came back a couple more times to visit over the next two months. I maintained a low profile and kept up with my probation, taking a weekly urinalysis and always coming up negative.

Approximately three months later the abandonment papers went through and my divorce from Kevin was final. It felt good when it was done, but it had taken so long that I already considered myself divorced way before then. This just legally finalized things. It didn't make me feel safe, though. At the end of the day, it was just a piece of paper, which didn't make me feel that he couldn't still find me or touch me. However, I did have one good consolation: this was an important step in starting my new relationship with Tom.

With a sense of anticipation, I arrived back home in New Jersey ready to start a new life with my fiancé. After I'd been home for a few days, I stopped by my old employers, Shakers and Satin Dolls, but I didn't take the stage. I'd already had my last dance. I could feel in my heart that my dancing career was over. Ending it was actually easier than I thought. I imagined I would miss the spotlight, but that wasn't the case. Just like an athlete who hangs up his jersey and cleats when he retires, I hung up my stilettos for the last time.

11

FROM PRADA
TO NADA

After I said good-bye to dancing and married Tom, I quickly made the transition to socialite. I put on a dress that went down to my knees and sensible heels to go to the country club with Tom and his family on weekends and look the Stepford wife part. However, underneath the conservative outfit I was still me. I wasn't ashamed of being a former exotic dancer, but Tom didn't feel comfortable when I told people where we had met.

Tom's mother, Dorothy, told me that she liked that I was different from everybody else and encouraged me to be myself. She welcomed me into the family with open arms. She had seven children and often told me that I reminded her of Pat (her daughter and Tom's sister), who had passed away in her thirties and had been the entertainer in the family. Mom Staub loved my spirit and I enjoyed her company. She brought a lot to the table as a woman, mother, and human being, and she taught me so much through our conversations over the years.

As we settled into married life, Tom kept saying that he couldn't wait to get me pregnant, and it was almost as if he wished it and it came true. While we both wanted to have a baby, we never thought it would happen that quickly—my getting pregnant with Christine was a complete surprise for Tom and me, to say the least. We were just going about being newlyweds, and then, all of a sudden, we were expectant parents.

My first pregnancy was rough. I basically set up shop in our bathroom and didn't leave for the first three months. I laid my pillow and blanket on a gymnastics mat on the floor, which served as sort of a bed. I'd be sick to my stomach in the bathroom when Tom would head off to work in the morning. He'd leave me some saltines and ginger ale to help my stomach, and I'd be sleeping on the bathroom floor or throwing up when he returned home at the end of the day. I was actually losing weight instead of gaining it.

Despite my discomfort, Tom and I got totally involved in our roles as expectant parents. We were both so excited. We bought lots of baby-name and pregnancy books and shopped for nursery furniture together. We interviewed pediatricians. We even went to Lamaze classes together. As I look back, I think Tom and I were probably the closest during this time.

One day, I got word that Kevin was living close by in New Jersey. I was going to be a mother soon, and with a new family developing, I had a lot to be grateful for and protect. My husband and I spoke at great length, and we decided to change my identity by legally changing my name from Beverly to Danielle. We contacted my lawyer and he took care of the paperwork for the name change. In April 1993, I legally became Danielle Staub. Previous reports have falsely claimed that I changed my name to hide from my past in Florida and the people who were involved in my court case. I changed my name to hide from one person only—Kevin Maher.

On December 4, 1993, our daughter Christine was born. It wasn't an easy birth, but when the doctor handed me my newborn Christine, everything was peaceful and perfect. I had a roomful of nurses and doctors attending me, but I was oblivious to it. I was holding my miracle, my baby. She was so big—nearly ten pounds—and healthy, and her skin was glowing, just as beautiful as it comes. Tom and I were happy. He couldn't wait to bring his family home.

I took my journey into motherhood very seriously. Children are like little sponges, and I wanted Christine to absorb all that is good in life to mold and shape her into a strong girl with a kind heart and a bright mind. When she was born, I woke up eager to begin every day with a new purpose. I now had a little girl who was looking to me for answers and guidance, and I was not going to steer her wrong or let her down. I was, and still am, a very protective mother. For the first eight weeks it was difficult for me to allow anyone to touch Christine, much less hold her. I was afraid that someone might drop her, hurt her, or touch her inappropriately. I was determined to witness everything she experienced because those first weeks of life are so uncertain. Not to mention, this is a bonding period between a mother and her newborn child. That was my time to learn my baby's sounds and language without words. And most important, I wanted to enjoy every moment and just breathe her in. It was exhausting, but a lot of fun and very important to me. Oh how I adored rocking with my baby until she would fall asleep in my arms.

I had the chance to show Christine a significantly different life than the one I had growing up. I recognized that motherhood was a blessing, an opportunity, and a second chance. This moment was not only the beginning of life for my young daughter, but a new beginning for me. It was a chance to move on from the past with great success as a passionate mother, wife, and homemaker.

Almost immediately after Christine's birth, Tom and I started trying to have another baby. I figured that if we tried then, in a year I would be pregnant and Christine would have a brother or sister by the time she was two years old. It seemed like the perfect plan.

However, I couldn't seem to get pregnant.

Tom and I were planning our sex life around the time of the month that I was the most fertile. I started cycles of fertility drugs and was going for regular shots and hormone therapy in conjunction with getting embryos implanted in my uterus at St. Barnabas hospital. It was a lot to go through on a daily basis and Tom was right there with me. That was why it was shocking to me to discover that while he was allowing me to put my body through all of this so that we could have another baby, Tom was having an affair. He was saying all along that his sperm couldn't have been the reason we weren't conceiving. After all, we had no problems conceiving Christine. So finding out that Tom's sperm count was abnormally low for a married man with—presumably—one partner, was a tough pill to swallow. There was no other explanation.

Soon after this discovery, Tom and I decided to take a long weekend together in New York City to talk things over. We booked a room at the Four Seasons and left Christine with our nanny.

Trust had been broken in our marriage, and Tom felt terrible about it. He owned up to what he had done like a man and promised it wouldn't happen again. I believed him and wanted to work through this tough time together. I was truly in love with my husband and wanted to have another baby with him. We both wanted to keep the family together.

That night in the city, we met up with Tom's brother, Jerry, and his wife, Denise, at the Rainbow Room for dinner and dancing. Normally, I can drink Cristal Rose and eat healthy portions of caviar. However, when the waiter brought the champagne and caviar to the table, I suddenly got nauseated from the smell.

I told everyone that I didn't feel well and excused myself to go to the restroom. Once inside, I met a couple of women, both mothers, who told me that I did not look well. I nodded and immediately ran into a stall to throw up. When I came out, one of the women said, "You're pregnant."

"No, I'm *not* pregnant," I responded with certainty. "I have been trying for three and a half years and it hasn't happened."

"Nope, you're pregnant," she said with a smile.

When Tom and I got back to our hotel room, I sent out the bell captain to a local twenty-four-hour pharmacy to get me some pregnancy-test kits. I spent the rest of the night in the bathroom peeing on the test sticks. Tom eventually fell asleep, and at about six in the morning, I let out a scream of happiness. Tom came charging into the bathroom, still half-asleep, and said, "Where's the spider?" (He knows I can't stand spiders and thought he had to kill one for me.)

I held up the positive test. "It's pink!" I yelled with excitement.

"Does this mean what I think it means?!"

"Yes!"

"Great, sweetie! Can I go back to bed now?" He meant it in a kind way, and later that day we celebrated the good news over brunch.

Jillian was born two weeks early, on May 14, 1998. When

Christine came into my hospital room to meet her new baby sister, I smiled at Tom and everything seemed to be glorious in our lives once again. With two beautiful daughters born out of love, I couldn't help but think how life could not get any better than this.

For the next four years, I lived a dream life. I had two beautiful and healthy daughters. I had everything materially that any woman could ever wish for. I could shop for designer clothes and shoes every day. At the drop of a hat, I could travel first-class anywhere in the world I wanted. I never had to worry about paying any of the bills; they were all paid on time or months in advance. Tom and I didn't owe a penny on our $2 million home. We bought brand-new luxury cars with cash anytime we wanted. My husband believed that you should never take out a loan; he was convinced that you should pay for everything in cash because you saved money on interest that way. His philosophy, which had been passed down by his father, was that if a person couldn't pay for something in full, then he or she shouldn't buy it.

Tom and I hosted old-Hollywood-style extravagant parties at our palatial New Jersey home. Semiformals would be held often and put together by professional party planner Amy Winters. Hundreds of invitations would be sent out, tents would be set up on the grounds three weeks in advance, and a dance floor would be specially built in our backyard. Valets and waiters dressed in tuxedos would stand at attention. Our social events always seemed like something right out of a movie. The flowers alone, arranged throughout the house, would cost $35,000.

However, while I was clearly comfortable financially, I wasn't happy emotionally. My marriage to Tom was not healthy. Tom created a lot of distance between us. Our date nights on Saturdays became less and less frequent. The communication between us was disintegrating. We no longer laughed together. We became two people living separate lives under the same roof.

From the outside it seemed as if we had everything. But on the inside, our relationship was hollow. It was no longer a marriage of love, and I wasn't about to live a lie or stay in a marriage because a man was taking care of me and making things easy. Should I have stayed in a marriage because all of my bills were paid? Should I have stayed in a marriage because I could buy anything I wanted? No, because that's what a prostitute does. I apologize, but it's true. Some women can live like that, but I was not going to be one of them. I refused to be one of them. Which is why being called a prostitute is so ridiculous to me— it is the opposite of what I really am.

Accepting that my marriage was over was really difficult. Tom was and is the father of my children, and it would have been so much easier to stay together for their sakes. I knew it would be hard for my daughters not to have a father around. They were still so young! Jillian was only four years old at the time our marriage was crumbling, and she needed a father at home to read to her and tuck her into bed every night. But ultimately I asked myself, *If I stay in this marriage, what example will I be setting for Jillian and Christine in the long run?* I imagined not a good one.

My inner voice was telling me things were wrong, and I needed to listen to it and be strong. After our last party, which we held to celebrate Christine's first Holy Communion when she was eight years old, the marriage was done. Tom and I couldn't mend our relationship and find our way back to each other. So, I filed for divorce.

Going through my divorce from Tom was when the real day-to-day struggles began for me. Paying all of the bills for a house the size of mine was completely foreign to me. Prior to being married, I owned and rented small homes, condos, and apartments. I had no idea what it cost to maintain a dwelling like the one in which I was living. I was now a mother of two and wasn't going to go back to dancing in clubs. That was in the past. I needed to reinvent myself in the present while I dealt with the challenge of making ends meet for my family.

Unfortunately, the bills didn't come to me—they went to my ex-husband, and he didn't always take care of them on time. It's difficult enough being a single mom, let alone having someone else in charge of the money. As a result, I started out behind the eight ball.

I had to pull in the reins. We went from going out to see a movie once a week to staying home and renting a movie once a month. I went from having a black American Express card to bringing buckets of change collected from under couch cushions and beds to the bank in exchange for paper money. I'd go to the supermarket with just $20 to feed three people. (Let's just say that macaroni and cheese became a big hit in our house.)

I had always felt for single moms, but when I became one, I found a new respect for them. I don't think it's any different being a single mother who lives in a house the size of mine or one who resides in a smaller dwelling. Wealthy or poor, no single mom out there has it easy.

Regardless, I had to create some sense of normalcy at home for my daughters' sakes. It was hard enough for them to lose a father, but they also underwent a complete change of lifestyle. I needed to find fun things that we could do together that didn't cost much money. For instance, each Saturday we would go into New York City. We didn't have enough money to pay to park in a garage, so we made friends with a street vendor on the Upper West Side who would kindly save a parking spot for me every Saturday. I don't how he saved the spot, but he came through every time! He'd even put change in the parking meter while my daughters and I would go off to Central Park and the American Museum of Natural History. We'd walk all over the city for hours. Christine and Jillian were used to riding door-to-door in our own limousine, and now they traveled everywhere on foot, but they didn't miss it at all.

Through these hard times, my daughters and I bonded with one another, and I'd even say that we had a blast together. We all developed a better understanding of one another and created a closeness that I wouldn't give up for anything. My daughters and I are best friends. While my marriage was coming apart, my daughters were the glue that kept me together.

To my surprise, as I adapted to my new roles, I became the complete opposite of who I originally was. I used to be concerned with things like "Where will I plug in my blow-dryer?" and I would send concierges out to buy me things; now I was cutting wood and building fires with my daughters. Simple pleasures became our daily pleasures. I stepped down from the proverbial high horse that my husband had put me upon and actually achieved things by myself. Who knew?

When a wife files for divorce and becomes a single mom, often her soon-to-be ex-husband puts her through hell. As I was going through my divorce, I spoke to many women who were wealthier than I was who came crashing down financially and emotionally. During the time we were separated, Tom asked me many times to get back together with him. I always said no, and I believe that fueled some of the difficulties of our divorce settlement. He was hurt by the rejection, and I can understand that. I knew we were a family. Trust me, many times I would say to myself, *What am I doing? I am still in love with Tom. Maybe I should get back together with him. Maybe I should give our marriage one more try.* But in my heart of hearts, I knew that getting back together with him wouldn't be for the right reasons. I would be going back because he could pay the bills. I was truly torn, and I cried often. I had been with Tom since my late twenties and we had shared many great moments together. Were there more to come? Possibly.

However, I knew that going back wasn't an option for me. I was looking ahead. But even though Tom may have learned his lesson when I filed for divorce and he lost me, I hadn't yet learned mine. I believe I'm finally learning it now.

———

After my divorce, I imagined that dating again couldn't be all that different. Wow, was I wrong!

The dating scene had dramatically changed. These days, it's tough to find a nice guy when you're in your twenties, let alone in your forties. Trying to date is hard enough when you have no kids, and I was a mother of two. Nights out on the town are few and far between when you're a single mom. The odds were not in my favor, but I was still hopeful that I could once again find love in my life.

Since I clearly wasn't going to meet anyone anywhere except maybe a car-pool lane, a few of my friends suggested that I hit up the Internet to find a guy. They told me to check out the dating website WealthyMen.com. While the name of the site certainly had a nice ring to it, I was skeptical about meeting men online. I had never done it before and it felt like a bit of a desperate move to me (not to mention I didn't even have an e-mail address). However, with limited time on my hands, I realized I should probably just give it a try. I signed up and posted my profile and photo online, but I wouldn't e-mail guys unless they contacted me first.

Almost instantly, my in-box was filled with messages from male cyber suitors. While I had no e-mails from the likes of Donald Trump, some of the men were successful and not bad-looking at all. I met a few interesting men on the site, and one in particular struck a chord with me, Johnny. He became my most significant relationship after Tom to date.

Johnny, better known as Goumba Johnny, used to play football for the New York Giants and Jets and has since become a stand-up comedian and DJ on the popular New York City radio station WKTU 103.5 FM. I had never listened to his show, but in e-mails, he seemed like a nice, smart guy. We corresponded heavily over the Internet for quite some time, then one day, while I was online, Johnny sent me a message telling me that I was really beautiful and he'd like to take me out to dinner.

I agreed to meet him for dinner in New Jersey one night when my daughters were visiting their father, and we had a great time together. Even though we had talked a lot over the Internet for months and I felt that I already knew him, clearly there was still more to learn. In person, over sangria, we shared a relaxed and easygoing vibe. More important, I proved to myself that even though I had owned this big house and lived a wealthy lifestyle for many years, underneath it all I was still the same girl who could let loose, hang out, and chill. It was just a matter of being with the right company, and right off the bat Johnny was just that. This was a good turning point for me.

Following dinner, I led Johnny back to the highway from the restaurant. Just when he was about to drive off, he lowered his car window, smiled, and said, "I miss you already. I can't wait to see you again." I thought that was sweet.

Johnny was a sweetheart, not complicated, and I enjoyed being in his company. We would have great conversations and talk every day, sometimes five times a day. He liked me for myself—he liked me best without makeup and in sweatpants. Johnny was also supergood to my kids. On Jillian's birthday, she even got to be on Johnny's radio show as a special treat.

Every Tuesday, Johnny would come over to the house after his broadcast. We called these Johnny Tuesdays, and we would all have dinner and then watch *House* on television. After the kids went to sleep, I would help him write his *Us Weekly* "fashion police" articles, in which he would provide comical comments about celebrity fashion don'ts.

Johnny and I probably had one of the more healthy relationships that I have ever been involved in. We trusted each other. I was totally honest with him about my past, and he was honest with me about his; he, too, had once been arrested and done time. His life now was on a very different path, and I was happy to be a part of it.

Well into our relationship, I was listening to Johnny's radio show one afternoon and Johnny's coanchor, Hollywood Hamilton, casually commented that Johnny had been at a professional hockey game the night before. Then Hamilton asked Johnny if he had brought a date with him to the game. Johnny didn't answer. Soon after this awkward moment over the airwaves, they cut to a commercial break. During the break, my phone rang. It was Johnny, asking if I was listening to his show. I told him no. He said that was good because something was said on the air that could be misconstrued, and he told me not to worry about it. *Don't worry about it?* I thought. *Seeing another woman is nothing to worry about?* But even though I was disappointed, I decided not to confront Johnny. I waited for three weeks for him to come clean on his own and explain. He never did, so I broke up with him.

After the breakup, Johnny called and said he wanted to get back together with me. He told me he missed me and wanted to see me again. I was reluctant at first, but I missed him, too. Yes, we had been lovers, but Johnny and I were also friends, and I missed our long talks. I had often spoken to him about marriage, and I wondered if maybe I had been rushing things a bit. Maybe I'd scared him off. Regardless, a trust had been broken between us and we needed to discuss it, so I made plans for him to come to the house for dinner when the children were visiting their dad.

The day before Johnny was supposed to come over to talk, I got a call from one of my friends, who offered their congratulations on my engagement to Johnny. This was news to me! I had no idea what they were talking about. The person explained that they had heard on Johnny's radio show that he had just gotten engaged to a girl named Danielle and assumed it was me because we had been seeing each other. "Well," I answered, "it's not this Danielle."

Here Johnny was planning on coming out to New Jersey to my home to repair our broken trust and he was already lying to me again. To think that I foolishly believed I might have scared him off by talking about marriage when he had just gotten engaged to someone else! I had no idea he was seriously dating somebody else at the same time he was dating me. Granted, the engagement was announced after we'd broken up, but he'd said he wanted to get back together with me. This was ridiculous! I had had enough. He was playing a game that I didn't want to play any longer. I called up Johnny and said, "Best of luck to you." It was time to say good-bye to Goumba!

———

After everything I went through with Johnny, I realized that romantic relationships with men were not going to be hugely significant in my life as I moved forward. Men were not going to define me. *I was going to define me!*

Men had become an unwelcome distraction. As I looked back on my life, while I had been in love and been loved at various times, what did it all add up to? Finding myself single and alone again. For better or worse . . . till death do us part . . . those weren't just words to me when I said them. They were vows of the deepest value based upon love, friendship, and equality. I was looking for the happily-ever-after in my life, and it became clear that I needed to create happiness within myself first.

Once again, I had reached another important crossroads. I was either going to move forward in a new direction or stay stuck in the path of certain destruction. The first step in moving forward was to take control of my life.

While my children have always come first, I still wanted to embark on a new career that would make them proud of me and instill some new pride in myself as well. Right around this time, the flyer for the casting of *The Real Housewives of New Jersey* came to my attention. While I was at first reluctant to be involved with the reality show, I soon realized that maybe this was the new beginning that I was looking for. Was my real life in suburban New Jersey interesting enough for television viewers? I wasn't sure. But when I began to look at the opportunity as a whole, I saw that it would not only mean I'd be working again and embarking on a new career, it would also enable me to spend more time with my daughters and help them further *their* dreams.

Joining the TV show also represented a chance to establish new friendships, with my castmates. I believed that we could all come together and show the world a new level of strength and understanding among women. As the only single mother in the cast, I would also have a unique voice and platform on the show, and I believed that my fellow castmates would become supportive girlfriends, allowing me to show single mothers of the world that we are not alone.

As the season progressed, I continued to be in the line of fire. Although the other women didn't know me that well, they seemed to dislike me very much, and eventually things came to a head. The women became determined to find out on their own what I was about, no doubt hoping to find something juicy, but through their "investigation" nothing but good things turned up in the past twenty-three years. So they had to dig beyond. They went back as far as 1986, when I was still practically a child. They judged me by things that happened far back in my past, at a time when we didn't even know one another and I hardly knew myself. The information in "the book" represented a chapter in my life that I closed a long time ago. In fact, when it was first published in 1996, the joint decision by my children's father and me was to take the high road by ignoring it. However, when it was presented on national television, I had no other choice but to address it.

Instead of recognizing that I had had the strength to walk away from an abusive relationship with an obsessed man, my castmates apparently wanted to bring me down for being involved with him in the first place. Instead of lifting me up and acknowledging my strength for changing my life after I got arrested, they *only* seemed to want to focus on that I was, in fact, arrested.

At first, I was upset and disappointed about how things

turned out on the show. I had believed these women were my friends, and it was a harsh way to learn the truth. I felt alone once again. But I soon realized that I wasn't alone at all. I began to get e-mails and letters from fans of the show who understood what I had been through in my life, and instead of judging me for it, they embraced me. They admired the strength and courage I had that allowed me to move on with dignity and change my life. Some had been through similar experiences with abusive men, and they wanted to let me know that they supported me. Even Charles Kipps, the author of "the book," recognized the kind of danger I had been in and my desire to move on from it. After the book was presented on the show, Kipps wrote an article in the *New York Post* on June 26, 2009, in which he stated, "No question, Beverly/Danielle now wants to forget Kevin, the man who brandished a Berretta [sic] at a strip joint because he thought she was cheating on him and dropped a bullet onto Beverly's forehead with the admonition: 'The next time you see one of these coming at you, it'll be coming at you a lot faster.'"

Despite having to go through some difficult moments on national TV, I'm grateful for what *The Real Housewives of New Jersey* represents to me. It has given me a platform whereby I can reach out to others who have been through similar experiences, and if I can help others by reliving the negative incidents of my life, then I will continue to find the strength to do so. The overwhelmingly positive response from the women and men who watch our TV show is encouraging. That kind of outpouring of understanding was not expected, but it has been well received and greatly appreciated.

Now I'm starting over yet again. But I've already done the hard part. This time I can exhale. I'm now an author and TV personality. I have been given a gift and a unique opportunity to communicate good things to others. *Positive* things. I will continue to do so. This book has been a journey for me to find and share the truth—*The Naked Truth*—and I'm blessed for it.

12

EMBRACE YOUR LIFE

believe that you have to learn to love yourself before you can truly love another. This has nothing to do with being conceited; it has to do with embracing yourself so you are putting out the kind of energy to the universe that you would like to receive for yourself in return. There are no mistakes. Only lessons. Choose to learn and move forward and embrace each lesson learned, for it's the experience you will grow from. During my life, I have continually learned the majority of my lessons the hard way. Some lessons were learned while I was locked up in a prison cell. Others lessons were learned while I was recovering in a hospital bed. Many lessons were learned when I was working as an exotic dancer. More recently,

I have learned new lessons from my experiences on national television.

I have been given not only a second chance in life, but a third, fourth, and maybe even more. These opportunities are extremely rare and I'm grateful for them. With each new lease on life I have learned so much along the way, and each time I reach a better understanding of myself.

I believe that you should not let the past define you. Embrace it, own it, then move on from it. If you are trying to deal with something bad that happened in your past, the best way is to dig deep within yourself, ask for forgiveness, and forgive yourself. If you are going through a rough time, know that you are exactly where you need to be. Once you get through it, you will get to the next level in life. You shouldn't think that whatever mistake you made or what you did wrong defines you as a person or your destiny. You define you. You get to choose your destiny. It is your path, your journey. Don't let anyone steer you away from your destiny. If you allow this to happen, you will have to travel the same path again and learn the same lesson twice.

I want to share a mantra of mine that reminds me of the most important lessons I've learned. I encourage you to learn it and repeat it as well:

Life is a gift
Love is a blessing
Trust is earned

Yes, I have made wrong decisions in my life. I have slipped and fallen hard many times. However, what counts is what we do when we muster up the strength to get up again, and move forward. I strongly believe that mistakes are only mistakes if we don't learn from them. When you have gone through all the experiences that I have, you can end up being consumed with negativity. However, it is a personal choice and I choose to be positive with all of my thoughts and actions.

Don't Look Now

Mirrors have never played a significant role in my life. I've never liked looking at myself. I used to be puzzled by why I didn't like to see my image up close, but I realize now that the reasons were much more complicated than I originally thought. They definitely weren't skin-deep.

My ongoing battle with the mirror began when I was young, and I feel it has a lot to do with the sexual and physical abuse that I was tormented by and that was left largely unresolved within me. When I looked at myself in the mirror as a teenager, I didn't see a whole person. I saw just a fragmented image of what I was supposed to feel like as a young girl. I thought I should see a young, happy, carefree teen blossoming into a woman, but instead I saw a fearful, lost, and confused person.

Sometimes looking at ourselves is the hardest thing we can

do. We try our best to put on a brave face for the world and the people around us, but when we are left alone to look at ourselves in the mirror, that moment of reality can often be difficult. Of course, I don't mean looking at oneself just in a physical sense. I'm talking about looking at the person who is revealed by looking into our own eyes and the moment of truth that occurs from deep within our souls when we do so.

I'm finally reaching a point where it has gotten much easier to look at myself in the mirror, and I think being on the television show and writing this book have certainly helped. These two platforms have allowed my voice to be heard and have enabled me to confront the issues of my past that I've avoided for so long.

Until now, I suffered from guilt and shame for many years because of the abuse that occurred during my childhood. However, through healing and self-discovery, I have finally realized that the abuse was not my fault. It should be the abusers who find it difficult to look at themselves in the mirror, not me. I hold my head high and am proud for having had the strength to survive all that I've gone through. I've found my way out of the darkness that others created and am now living in love and light.

If you've been through any of the types of abuse that I've been through, I encourage you to be proud when you look at yourself in the mirror. Hold on to the truth that *it wasn't your fault* that you were abused as a child. You didn't do anything wrong. There's no need to carry shame. Let go of the past and move forward to the future. Remember, this is your life, so live it your way. Now you can look at yourself in the mirror and smile.

What's Love Got to Do with It?

When it comes to love, I have received many mixed messages throughout my life. When my abusers would sneak into my room in the middle of the night and tell me to keep quiet as they violated me, they didn't love me. How could they? They didn't even love themselves. For a young child, the feeling of being safe is one of the essential foundations of love, and I never felt safe. Not once.

Later, I was in many relationships with men who told me that they loved me, but I wondered why I was still in so much pain. I felt empty. Please recognize your self-worth and leave an abusive relationship before it's too late. I beg you. If you think that it's easier to just stay in it, you're wrong. If you think that he or she will change, he or she won't. If you think things will get better by themselves, they don't. If you try to leave and your partner won't leave you alone, seek protection. Go to the authorities. Ask friends and family for help. Many people think that breaking up with a partner is a personal defeat—it isn't. By staying in an abusive relationship, you're just defeating yourself every day that you're still there.

So, what's love got to do with it? Everything. Love gets you up in the morning and motivates you to tackle the challenges of the day. Love puts you to bed at night and lets you sleep easily. In a healthy relationship, love is supposed to make you feel free, not like a captive. We all have a choice when it comes to love. We can choose not to be abused and seek out true love. We can choose not to be afraid to be alone and know that love will eventually find us. But it's up to you to make the right decisions in your life that will open up the doors and allow love to find you.

Find Yourself First

True love exists. That fairy-tale relationship of a man and a woman and the happily-ever-after is out there for all of us. I still believe that my knight in shining armor will arrive one day soon. He will appear in all of his glory and we will be together for the rest of our lives. Why hasn't he arrived yet? Because of me.

I have had many relationships. While some seemed right at the moment, in the end I wasn't with the right partners. If I had been, I would still be with one of them right now. Quite honestly, I think they were holding me back from finding my true love. After a breakup, many people—myself included—tend to jump immediately into another relationship. We believe that's better than being alone. It fills a void. But inevitably the next relationship becomes a rebound relationship. Are you as tired as I am of going from rebound to rebound? Well, I've found that the only way for this cycle to stop is for you to stop it.

The quick fix and the Band-Aid on the heart seems like an easy way to go, but in the long run, it isn't. You need to get to the root of the problem of why your relationship failed. I think that more often than not, the root of the problem is you.

I believe that, to find true love, you need to find yourself first.

I think when you're comfortable and being the best version of yourself, you will attract the best partner for you. When you've found a way to completely love yourself, that's when the glow comes from within and the rest of the world takes notice. Taking the time to work on yourself and your issues will put you in position to be able to tackle a real relationship, one of substance.

I have put in a lot of time both personally and professionally working on myself, and I fully realize that I have more work to do. I am a work in progress. But I believe I am now entering a place where I will be able to accept my true love. He may not be perfect. He may even have been through a few marriages that didn't last, just as mine didn't. However, if two people focus on themselves first and do the work they need to do to come into their own, in the end they will be with each other for the right reasons.

Tearing Down to Rebuild

When I was married to Tom, even though I had complete financial freedom, I wasn't really free. Even though I had peace of mind with regard to the financial side of things, I didn't have peace regarding a truly loving relationship. For women, this is one of the most important things in life, and I urge you all to realize it. The mindset of putting up with what you *don't* want in a relationship because you have financial security is really selling yourself short . . . or, just plain selling yourself. You need to learn to love and respect yourself the way you want other people to. This rule applies to friends and loved ones alike.

A lot of men and women seem to settle for someone just for the sake of having another person there. What people don't realize is that you're allowing a person to occupy a space in your life that doesn't really belong to them. People think it's better than being lonely, when in essence you're screaming out to the universe you have what you need when you really don't. It's full. Slot taken! It's the same thing with love. If you keep your love life vacant, while you work on everything else about yourself, that place reserved for love will eventually be occupied by the right person. I've learned through my spiritual work how to set the bar high and to keep it there. I have had opportunities, but I've chosen not to go down just any road. What I've decided is that I'm going to have it all. I deserve it all. So I asked myself, "How can I get there?"

I learned that before you can reconstruct, you have to tear

down the structure first. What I am referring to is breaking down all of the walls that are not built correctly and starting fresh so that your life has a solid foundation. The first step is to do a purging of your spirit. Once you get your spirit healthy and uncluttered, all else will fall into place, including love. But you can't do it all at once. You have to build with baby steps. You don't just start running, and believe me, I wanted to! I had to give up complete control of my life. Turn your life over to a higher being. In my case, I turned it over to God. Remember, faith walks in when all doubt walks out the door. Send doubt packing, and negativity will follow. Allow only the positive in.

The Climb

Until recently, when my daughter Jillian wrote me two original songs, my favorite song was "The Climb" sung by Miley Cyrus. When I heard the lyrics, they really hit home with me: "Ain't about how fast I get there. Ain't about what's waiting on the other side. It's the climb." Miley is right. It *is* all about the climb.

I'm as guilty as the next person of pushing and striving to get to that next level of success in my life as fast as I possibly can. But when we become so focused on reaching our personal goals and career destinations, we forget about the journey it took to get us there. Getting to the top can be more enjoyable and even more memorable than the success itself.

For me, the climb represents the journey as well as the little details and special moments that mean so much along the way. When you reach the success you aspire to and look back on your life, I think it's important to pause and ask yourself, How did I get here? Who helped me along the way? What did I have to sacrifice? What was the meaning of it all? I have learned in life to slow down and take one step at a time. Once you have completed the necessary measures, you can move on to the next step.

There will probably be many obstacles and speed bumps along the way as you make your climb. I think that's inevitable. But I think you should try not to sell the bad times short because you can learn from those experiences and grow from them as a person. Don't forget the sleepless nights of worrying. They are a part of your climb that helps build character, which can last a lifetime. You're sure to learn from your bad decisions as well as your good ones.

We all have a set of goals and dreams that we hope to conquer, both professionally and personally. But we can never forget the road we take that gets us there. It's important to enjoy the journey just as much as the final destination.

Like Attracts Like

At times in my life I wasted my time asking, "Why me?" as opposed to addressing the real issue. I also wasted a lot of time blaming others for negative things that were happening to me. In time, I realized that one of the reasons these things were happening was *me*—it wasn't just fate. For many years I was in a negative place and was attracting negative people and experiences into my life. Since then I've discovered that whatever a person puts out into the universe—whether it be negative or positive—will come right back to him or her. It's called manifestation, and my energist, Sarai Salinas, taught me all about it. She is my personal trainer for my spirit.

She told me that energy is just like a boomerang—what you put out into the universe will come right back to you—and light attracts light, while darkness attracts darkness. By extension, love attracts love, and hate attracts hate.

I believe that our thoughts are much more powerful than you may think, and that you *will* what you want into your life. Therefore, if you think of really good things, guess what happens? Really good things come to you. The flip side is just as true. If you believe that you will be poor, loveless, and unhappy, there is a good chance you will be. It is that simple.

I find that it takes a lot less energy to be happy and positive than it does to be sad and negative. By talking to positive people who are making things happen, I think you will accomplish much more in your life. If you catch yourself thinking negatively, it's time to switch gears immediately. If you're in a positive place and someone starts talking negatively about someone or something, don't feed into it. Change the conversation or change your location. I've found that when I stay positive, everyone else usually follows. Here is another mantra of mine that I encourage you to repeat:

If it feels good
Draw it near
If it does not
Steer clear

Surrender Without Giving Up

I came to the point in my life where it was essential to surrender to everything except positive thoughts. And I am going to tell you right now that you can't begin to imagine how difficult it was. It's one of the hardest things I have ever done. When I entered on a spiritual path, I had to stop forty-seven years of thinking negative thoughts. I also had to get rid of the "victim" mentality.

When you surrender in this way, you're *not* giving up. You are just not giving in to all of the negative things that come across your path and into your mind. Choose to stay in the light because the darkness will bite you in the ass! When someone does something negative to you, don't retaliate (darkness). Instead, surrender (light). Surrendering shows that you have faith. Understand that others who do negative things will get what they have coming to them. Don't get in the way of karma taking its natural course. Karma is a force and it's coming. As I often say, karma is a bigger bitch than I am!

For many, it's much easier to be negative and to attack others instead of looking within oneself and fixing what makes you so unhappy. People who are truly happy do not attack one another. It's all a façade. Once you raise your awareness, you'll realize what a vicious cycle negativity is and steer clear of it. You might not see any end in sight now, but you have to surrender and let things take their course. Once you do, you will build up the strength to manifest what is rightfully yours, which are all of your hopes and dreams.

Go Through the Darkness to Get to the Light

I know a lot about the darkness. It's a force that can consume you. I was there and I never plan on returning. But if I hadn't gone through my past I couldn't be where I am today—and let me tell you, that was one of the hardest journeys that I ever had to make. I compare getting it out of your life to the last push of childbirth. It's going to be painful, but as soon as you make it through that final push, you get the most glorious gift of your life.

It took age and perspective for me to realize that I had to go through the darkness from my childhood to become who I am today. I have no regrets. When I look at my daughters

I realize now it was all worth it. And when we look into one another's hearts no words are necessary. I know I have their absolute trust. Here's the thing—I *had* to experience what I did in order for my children not to. So I can tell them point blank, "I've been there. I've done that. And we're not going down that path again."

When I see people being negative around me, I sense darkness consuming them and it's almost as if they've opened a bottle of toxins. You don't breathe in toxins. You keep a cap on it. Once you open the bottle and the negativity/toxins escape, it gets ugly. Part of the reason I feel that I can classify myself as a great mom is that my children tell me so, and the other part is that I work very hard at keeping the toxins and negativity tucked away. Do I slip up every once in a while? Of course, I'm human. I'm still learning daily how to steer clear of negativity. But the moment I see the darkness coming I push it away and put the cap back on the bottle.

You can only recognize the darkness when you step out of it. Life experience has taught me that it's much better to move forward than back. So let them keep each other in the darkness while we live in love and light.

EPILOGUE

want to deeply thank you for reading my book and taking this journey alongside me. I know that it has been a long adventure, filled with many ups and downs, and one that has perhaps been difficult for some of you to read. I assure you that it was difficult for me to put it down on paper.

As I was writing this book, I had to go back to some dark places in my past, which were at times overwhelming to revisit. Some days during the writing were far more painful than I ever imagined they would be. I recalled times when I felt shame and moments when I experienced fear. I had to relive disturbing and disappointing episodes that I'd tucked away and hoped not to speak about ever again, let alone share with the public. However, knowing that you were willing to go there with me really helped.

When I sat down to write, I decided that I was no longer going to pretend to be someone I wasn't. I wanted to stop being everything to everyone and take a moment to write this book and heal myself. I was determined to finally come out of the darkness that had imprisoned me for such a long time. For too long, I doubted that this could ever be done. I was afraid that facing these things would destroy me. However, what I have discovered is quite the contrary.

When I first began to talk about my past on national television, I was astonished at the number of people who approached me and thanked me for finding the strength to talk about my experiences. They told me that I was a voice for them, and that is what motivated me to write this book. They gave me the strength to keep moving forward when it was difficult to do so, and I wanted to show others that they, too, could reach within themselves the way I had and achieve growth through healing. I wanted to step out of the darkness, reveal some of the problems that they might have gone through, and encourage them to become who they are meant to be. If I can accomplish this for even one other person through this book, then revisiting my painful past has been worth it. It means a victory not only for myself but for the people who are misunderstood and have been suffering.

This isn't the end of my story by any means. This is the beginning and I will continue my journey in the positive. I have never been known to be the silent type. Being on a reality television show helped me to avoid being quiet and pushed me to face the painful truth that has been with me all of these years. Sharing my life with others has empowered me. I realized that you have to go through darkness to get to the light.

ACKNOWLEDGMENTS

often say, "It takes a village." These are the people I hold the nearest and dearest to my heart. Every blessing.

Christine and Jillian, my daughters, you have sacrificed so much and never wavered from your love, support, and kindness toward me. Words can only begin to express how grateful and proud I am to be your mom. You are both truly the biggest blessings in my life.

Paradise, Fendi, and Sasha, my adorable Chihuahuas, who are always happy to see me and love me no matter what.

Ruth Merrill, a beloved mother and grandmother. I hope you are resting peacefully with my brothers. Thank you for being my angel in heaven. I love you and miss you.

Steven Priggé, thank you for going on this journey with me. Living my life was difficult, but writing it down for all to read was even tougher. I could not have imagined writing my memoir with anyone other than you. You are a gifted writer and have become a dear friend.

Sarai Salinas, my energist and dearest friend, thank you for helping put together the broken pieces of my spirit. I believe in angels and I have one in you.

Ronnie Arthur Merrill and all of my deceased brothers, you may have lost your battle with cystic fibrosis, but I feel you helping me in my life every day.

Dorothy and Bill, you have been like a mother and father to me. Rest in peace, Mom Staub.

Tom, thank you for being part of my life and sharing in the births of our two beautiful daughters.

Danny Williams, my cousin and friend, who has been like a brother to me. Thanks for giving me a place to lean when we were kids.

Father Michael Lombardo of Our Lady of Consolation, I'm very blessed to have you in my life. You teach me through love and patience how to cope with some of life's trials. You have shown me in so many ways how to be a better person, mother, and friend. My kids and I look forward to Mass every Sunday, mainly because of you. Thank you and God bless.

Tommy DeRosa, you are now and always will be my best friend. You've been there through it all and never changed your position in my life. Thank you for giving me a place to rest my head and being Uncle Tommy to my daughters. Love to Rob as well.

Jorge, you are and always will be an example of what a

true gentleman represents. Thank you for being a part of my journey.

Norman Elliott Kent, thank you for giving me back my freedom and believing in me throughout all of these years and beyond.

Theresa Van Vliet, thank you for risking it all to stand firmly by my side. Instead of prosecuting me, you recommended freedom.

Judge Eugene Spellman, may you rest in peace. I will never forget your words to me.

Maureen Beirne, a special thanks to my very best childhood friend. You will always be a part of me.

John Molinelli, thank you for your guidance, advice, and friendship during this past year.

Joe Kilmer, thank you for proving to me that friendships can last a lifetime.

Peter Flint, thank you for being not only my acting coach but one of my dearest friends till this day.

Vinnie Potestivo, you inspire me to be my very best. Thank you for loving my children as well.

Eric Alt, thank you for being a wonderful friend and my brilliant hair colorist.

Andrew Capone, thank you for being my first breakout mentor and advising me, and I quote, "Before you save the world, feed your children." The children are fed. Can I save the world now? Special thanks to your wife, Cynthia.

Ivan Bart, thank you for recognizing Christine's beauty and

using your expertise in developing her career. My daughter is in great hands.

Brian Nash, thank you for being an inspiration to my daughter Jillian and helping her to develop her art and voice in music into something more than fabulous.

Jacqui "JJ" Phillips, thank you for being a good friend and my talented makeup artist.

Mary Jane Piccinich, thank you for being a constant calm energy in my family's lives and for doing the best nails ever.

Frank Vincent, thank you for patiently guiding me in the right direction and reminding me to enjoy the ride.

Maria L. Gattuso, thank you so much for the laughter and positive energy.

Kim Schumann, my attorney, thank you for giving me back the ability to express my life experiences in this book. For defending me and my honor, I'm eternally grateful.

Mark Turner and Maura Teitelbaum at Abram Artists, thank you both for recognizing my potential and helping me bring it to fruition. I'm a work in progress.

Thank you to the entire team at Simon & Schuster. Anthony Ziccardi, thank you for your enthusiasm right out of the gate in our first meeting. Patrick Price and Emily Westlake, my editors, thank you for understanding me on so many levels and staying true to *The Naked Truth*.

Sirens Media Group, Rebecca Toth, and Lucilla D'Agostino, special thanks for finding me a few years ago and asking me to do a show called *The Real Housewives of New Jersey*.

ACKNOWLEDGMENTS

To the team at Bravo, thank you for recognizing that I had a little something extra to give and supporting my decision to write my life story. A special thanks to Lenid, Gil, Jacob, Dave, and the entire crew on season 2 of *RHONJ*. Christian Barcellos, thank you for supporting me from the start. Kristen Anderson, thank you for your professionalism and for always treating me as an equal. Andy Cohen, thank you for knowing that I believe in you as you believe in me.

Ian Drew of *Us Weekly*, thank you for being in my corner right from the start, and I am proud to call you my friend.

Kathy, Emil, and Patrice Innocenti, thank you for being so supportive of me and all my endeavors.

Danny Provenzano, thank you for your friendship.

The Cystic Fibrosis Foundation (CFF), you are helping to make changes every day to strive toward a better tomorrow for those who are affected by this debilitating disease. Live, love, and breathe.

A special thank you to all my friends in Wayne, New Jersey, where I have lived since 1993.

All of my friends and fans on Facebook and followers on Twitter, thank you to each and every one of you.

ABOUT THE AUTHORS

DANIELLE STAUB is the breakout star of Bravo's hit reality television series *The Real Housewives of New Jersey*. She has numerous projects in the works, including a fitness and nutrition video, T-shirt line, and another book, perhaps. When she's not working on her own career, she manages her two daughters' careers. During her downtime, she loves being a mom as well as staying busy with her local parish and various charities. For more information, visit www.danielle-staub.com.

STEVEN PRIGGÉ is a New Jersey–born entertainment journalist as well as an author and coauthor of numerous books. For more information, visit www.stevenprigge.com.